A Guide to the Buddhas

A Guide to the Buddhas

Vessantara

Windhorse Publications

Originally published as Parts 1 and 2 of *Meeting the Buddhas* 1993
Revised text published as *A Guide to the Buddhas* 2008

Published by Windhorse Publications Ltd
11 Park Road
Birmingham
B13 8AB
UK

Printed by The Cromwell Press Ltd, Trowbridge, England

Cover image: Śākyamuni Buddha painting by Aloka
reproduced by permission of Padmaloka Retreat Centre

British Library Cataloguing in Publication Data
A catalogue record for this book is available from the British Library

ISBN 978 1 899579 83 9

Contents

Illustrations

Colour

Monochrome

About the Author

Vessantara is a senior member of the Western Buddhist Order. Born Tony McMahon in London in 1950, he gained an MA in English at Cambridge University. He became interested in Buddhism in his teens, and first had direct contact with Buddhists in 1971. In 1974 he was ordained and given the name Vessantara, which means 'universe within'.

In 1975 he gave up a career in social work to become more involved with the development of the Friends of the Western Buddhist Order. Since then he has divided his time between meditating, studying, and assisting the development of several Buddhist centres, including retreat centres in England, Wales, and Spain.

Vessantara is much in demand as a Buddhist teacher. For seven years he led three-month courses for people entering the Order and now gives talks and leads retreats and workshops throughout Europe and Australasia.

He has written written several books, including *Tales of Freedom, The Mandala of the Five Buddhas, The Vajra and Bell*, and *Female Deities in Buddhism*.

Introduction

An English friend of mine went to Japan in his mid-teens to visit his sister who was working there. One day they made an excursion to Kamakura, a city in central Japan. There my friend saw his first Buddha. It was a giant bronze statue of the Buddha Amida (infinite light), which towers fifteen metres high. My friend was so overwhelmed by the calm power of this figure that, without ever having heard any Buddhist teaching, he knew he was a Buddhist.

Buddhism appeals to many people in the West because it uses reasoned argument. It is not dogmatic and requires no blind faith; instead it relies on common sense and empirical methods. However, rational understanding of the path to Enlightenment will not be sufficient to motivate us to follow that path to its end. When we attempt to transform ourselves in line with our rational ideals, we all too often encounter inner resistances. With our reason we may plot a path to the ideal. In our mind's eye we see it stretching into the distance like a railway track gleaming in the sunlight, its parallel lengths of steel arrowing along the straightest path towards our distant goal. However, when we try to follow the track we have laid down, we are likely to be beset by all kinds of difficulties. At some places we find ourselves sabotaged, derailed by protesting aspects of our personality that we had not consulted when we planned the line. At others we find the track washed away by floods of powerful feelings that we had not known existed. Again, we may become lost in fogs of confusion, not knowing why we ever set out on the journey in the first place.

To overcome these obstacles we have to involve our emotions and deeper energies in the quest for Enlightenment. To help us to achieve this, Buddhism uses not rational argument but the language of symbol, myth, and poetry to communicate its message to our depths. This 'second language' is highly developed in Buddhism and very effective. My friend's experience at Kamakura is a striking demonstration of this. The Buddha figure spoke to him so directly in the language of symbols that he needed hardly any rational convincing to become a Buddhist.

The fastest way to make progress on the path to Enlightenment is to learn both the language of reason and the language of symbol, myth, and poetry. In this way the message of human development will be communicated to our whole being, both head and heart, to our rational everyday mind, and to our unconscious depths.

A major part of the 'vocabulary' of this 'second language' of Buddhism is made up of archetypal figures which express aspects of Enlightenment. This book is an exploration of the main figures we are likely to meet in practising Buddhism in the West. All these figures can be visualized in meditation and devotional ritual in order to catalyse processes of inner transformation. Before meeting any of them, however, we need to look at what the word 'archetypal' means in this context, and why these figures are so important – how interacting with them can help us to fulfil our potential as human beings.

The word 'archetype' was popularized by Carl Jung, the Swiss analytical psychologist, though it is a rather 'shape-shifting' concept, which he never defined very precisely. In essence, an archetype is a deep mental patterning. When we encounter expressions of the archetypes – perhaps in our dreams – they often have a timeless quality, and a sense of 'meaningfulness', a heightened reality that is hard to explain rationally. It is as though they connect together and resonate with many threads of our experience. Archetypal material often feels transpersonal, as though one is tapping into experiences that go far into the past, and are common to all human beings. The basic experiences of humanity in all ages – such as the sun, moon, stars, father, mother, fire, wind, rivers and seas, birds, beasts, fish, and stones – form the building blocks of our experience of life. Dreams and myths which touch on such basic aspects of life as these are quite likely to have an archetypal quality.

Dwelling on something which acts as an archetypal symbol for us can produce deep changes within our minds. For instance, if we were to contemplate the sun, we should find far more happening than just a growing appreciation of the ball of gas 93,000,000 miles away. We should probably find that we were contacting an inner source of awareness, lighting up the darkness of unconsciousness, an organizing principle within our minds which draws other mental contents into a more harmonious pattern around it. Similarly, meditation on archetypal figures has far-reaching positive effects.

Over the centuries, thousands of archetypal figures have appeared within the Buddhist tradition. Each has a sense of coming from a realm of heightened reality. Each feels rich in symbolic meaning. However, they do more than constellate feelings associated with fundamental aspects of human life. They express, through colour and form, an experience that goes far beyond the range of normal human experience. They communicate the extraordinary experience of Enlightenment. There are a great number of these figures, because Enlightenment is like a jewel which can be looked at from different points of view. One is always looking at the same jewel, yet it has different facets, such as wisdom, compassion, peace, love, freedom, energy. Each of these figures brings us into contact with particular facets of Enlightenment.

Through interacting with these 'archetypes of Enlightenment' we can connect with and transform major streams of energy within our psyche. Not only that, we can make our ideals much more tangible. 'Wisdom', 'compassion', and 'Enlightenment' may sound fine, but they are still just concepts. When we meet with one or another of the Buddhist archetypal figures – whether in a painting or a sculpture or visualized in meditation – we are brought face to face with a being who embodies Enlightenment, whose smile warms us with compassion, and whose eyes shine with understanding of the nature of Reality. An encounter with such a figure is likely to move us far more deeply than a list of the qualities of someone who is Enlightened.

These figures do not just embody qualities such as wisdom and compassion. Each of the figures in this series of books can communicate a message to us about our potential as human beings. If we make the effort, we too can develop to a point where we understand the nature of Reality, put paid to all suffering, and feel an infinite care for all life. Thus each of these archetypal figures is a vision of what we can become. We are like seeds, and the Enlightened figures are the different types of flower into which we can grow.

It may be argued that these traditional Buddhist figures, which come from ancient India or Tibet, are not appropriate models for us as Westerners. However, there are considerable advantages to meditating on figures that are guaranteed by the tradition. Each has been found helpful in actual practice by Buddhist meditators over hundreds of years. In that sense they are all 'tried and tested'.

Even if the figures in this series are destined to change their outward forms and become more Western in appearance, as Westerners interested in Buddhism our first task is to explore the treasure-house of the tradition. In time to come, when we have understood the value of what we have inherited, we can then perhaps choose, in certain cases, to re-fashion some of the golden figures we have received into new forms, to place some of the jewels in a new setting.

In any case, with a little acquaintance these traditional figures need not seem strange or distant. After all, they are expressions of qualities and energies which with some exploration we can find very close to home. Each of these beautiful and compelling figures represents a potential of our own minds. In our depths, on the levels on which we shall experience Enlightenment, we are neither Eastern nor Western. These Buddhist figures are gateways to experiences that go far beyond our conditionings of culture, race, or gender. It is my hope that, through reading this book and coming to know these figures, something of that potential will be actualized.

One

The Fountainhead of Buddhism

Buddhism began with the Buddha, but it does not rest on or rely upon him. If it were to be proved that he was a mythical character (and historians are virtually unanimous that he was a real, historical figure), the path to Enlightenment would still exist. Universal impermanence would still be a fact, and wherever there is change there is always the potential for directing that changing process onto higher and higher levels. Buddhism could go on without the Buddha.

Yet for human beings there is always a special thrill about beginnings. We remember the 'first time'; we value newness; we honour the pioneer. Our consciousness registers any change in the patterns of life which may herald a new development, a new experiment in evolution – even if it is only the marketing of a new brand of breakfast cereal. Pioneers transcend national and racial boundaries. When Yuri Gagarin flew into space, he was Everyman, and he took us all with him.

So Śākyamuni, (Tibetan *Shakya Thup pa*) the historical Buddha, in whom Enlightenment first flowered in this historical age, will always be remembered and honoured by Buddhists. The story of his struggle and spiritual victory will continue to be told with gratitude, for without his efforts we would live in a darker and more confused world.

More than this, Śākyamuni's story has become what we could call the 'central myth' of Buddhism. The word 'myth' here does not mean something untrue; on the contrary, it means something of universal significance. Generations of Buddhists have dwelt on the events of this story and found that, even though they may be living in very different circumstances, it is still relevant to them. Over time, it has revealed many layers of meaning. In the Introduction we saw that Enlightenment has many facets which are expressed by the many different Buddhist figures. A large number of these were discovered by people meditating deeply on the life of Śākyamuni. Thus an account of these figures logically begins with his story.

When it comes to recounting the life of Śākyamuni, it is sometimes a problem to know with what order of reality we are dealing. Spiritual experience may have no obvious outward expression. To appreciate what is going on, we have to be able to enter the mind, the inner world, of the spiritual aspirant. Accounts of great Buddhist teachers often do this by externalizing inner spiritual events – representing them as events in the physical world. Sometimes it is not easy to decide what is literal fact and what is psychological or spiritual experience transposed into the key of the everyday. The events related are true, but it can be hard to decide to what order of truth, what level of consciousness, they belong. Cutting out all the elements of the story you suspect of being 'unreal' – i.e. non-historical – is to risk throwing out the Buddha with the bathwater.

In telling the story of Śākyamuni I have to select from among the many versions of the story – some seemingly 'factual', others with many incidents which cannot be taken literally. So I am telling *a* story of Śākyamuni, and I leave it to the reader to decide the order of reality of the different elements.

The Buddha's life

We have to go back 2,500 years, to what today is southern Nepal. At that time the region was peopled by the Śākya clan. The Śākyans comprised a small but proud republic, destined within fifty years to be swallowed up by one of their more powerful neighbours to the south. The elected ruler of the Śākyans was a man called Śuddhodana. He had a wife called Māyā, who died a few days after giving birth to their first child. Śuddhodana's grief at losing her mingled with joy that she had bequeathed to him a healthy son and heir.

The child was given the name Siddhārtha, to go with the family name of Gautama. He was brought up by his mother's sister, Mahāprajāpati, and soon showed himself to be an intelligent boy who could also distinguish himself in archery and other sports. The family were rich, and Siddhārtha lacked for nothing. There was a palace for the winter, a palace for the summer, and another for the rainy season.

All the time, Śuddhodana watched his strong, bright son with paternal pleasure and a certain unease. When the child was a few days old, an old man called Asita, with a reputation for prophecy, had come down from the mountains. Examining the baby, he had predicted a glorious future for him. He would either become a powerful world ruler or he would be a great sage, an Enlightened One. Śuddhodana had been delighted with the prophecy. However, he was a ruler and a statesman. He wanted his son to carry on the 'family business'. If Siddhārtha became a great world ruler, the Śākyans would have a glorious future. What, though, if the child followed the way of the sage? Another family would rule the Śākyans, and Śuddhodana would have no one to whom to pass on his experience, or the family wealth.

Śuddhodana observed his son carefully, encouraged when he proved adept at learning the laws and customs of the Śākyans, alarmed if he showed signs of hankering after the religious life. Śuddhodana did everything in his power to ensure that his son enjoyed life and was satisfied with it. He married him off to a beautiful young girl called Yaśodharā. He surrounded him with entertainments. He showered him with material goods.

Yet still Śuddhodana did not feel secure. It was not enough to ply his son with pleasures. To be quite sure, he needed to shield him from the suffering of the world, to cut the dark squares from the chessboard of life and hide them away. Śuddhodana therefore worked to keep his son separated from anything which would make him think deeply and start asking questions about the meaning of existence. He surrounded him with other young people, laughter, and amusements. He shielded him from all signs of suffering. Siddhārtha lived in the sort of world you find in some modern advertisements, in which everyone is rich, young, and surrounded by beautiful objects.

However, Śuddhodana's attempts to keep the world at arm's length from his son were doomed. Siddhārtha became bored with the pleasures of the palace, and started venturing out in his chariot – another beautiful toy given him by his father. As he did so he began to encounter strange sights. He saw people quite unlike his young and attractive companions in the palace. He saw someone bent over, shuffling along, her face wrinkled like an elephant skin. He saw someone lying in pain, unable to move, being tended by his relatives. He saw a lifeless body being carried away for disposal, just as his servants would whisk away a meal of which he had tired.

The story says that the young man had been so carefully sheltered by his father that in his whole life he had never seen anyone old or sick. He had never seen a corpse, or even been taught the word 'death'. Confronted with these disquieting sights he had to turn to his charioteer for information. The man was under orders from Śuddhodana just to keep Siddhārtha amused, but when questioned he had to concede that old age, sickness, and death were all parts of life, that there was no escaping them. He was even forced to admit that sooner or later Siddhārtha would experience them as well. On his return, Siddhārtha looked at his palace with sober eyes. He had imagined he was free, in a bright world. Now he had discovered that he was in the power of three forces who were just biding their time before asserting their sovereignty over him.

Siddhārtha became pensive and quieter than before. His wife was expecting a child, and it weighed heavily on him that not just he, but this infant, would become sick, grow old, and die. Everywhere he looked – at his musicians, his dancing girls, his servants, his beautiful wife, his beloved father – he saw change and death. An assassin had entered his palace, and life had lost its security.

One day, on another trip with his charioteer, Siddhārtha saw something and called to him to stop. Coming towards him was the most dignified man he had ever seen. He walked calmly through a busy thoroughfare, undisturbed by the clamour around him. He was not distracted by anything or anyone, but moved steadily and purposefully through the crowd, like an arrow that knows its target. The man was not finely dressed, he wore only the meanest of rag robes, yet his bearing was that of a nobleman. Siddhārtha hurried down from his chariot to question him. The calm man gently told him that he was a homeless wanderer. He had 'gone forth' from his home and family life to search for truth, to answer the riddles of existence.

It was not long before the charioteer managed to persuade Siddhārtha that it was time to return to the palace. However, this short conversation left its mark. Not just the conversation – the figure of the self-controlled wanderer walked across his dreams. It stood between him and the palace entertainers. It beckoned to him. The charioteer informed Śuddhodana what had happened, who was quick to notice the change in his son, his preoccupied air. Śuddhodana began to fear the worst. He set men to watch the palace gates at night.

Nonetheless, Siddhārtha's mind was made up. Even the birth of his son Rāhula made no difference. How could a father stand by and watch his son tortured by sickness, hobbled by old age, and executed by death? Rāhula, everyone, had to be rescued from these sufferings. Siddhārtha knew he would rescue no one by sitting in his palace getting fat. The time had come to leave, not for the sake of leaving, but in order to come back with an answer to the riddle of life, a cure for the troubles of humanity.

One full moon night, he stole out of the palace unseen. He took his horse, Kanthaka, and a servant, and made a dash for the border of the country, for he feared that, if discovered, Śuddhodana would have him brought back by force. It had not been easy to leave. He had not dared to take a last look at his sleeping wife and son. If he had done so he could never have brought himself to go. He rode to the bank of a river that marked the border of Śākyan territory. There he cut off his long, oiled locks with a sword, and swapped clothes with a beggar. He gave a message to his servant to take back to his family with Kanthaka, and walked off into the night.

Siddhārtha wandered anonymously from place to place. At first it was hard. He begged his food, and ate whatever was put into his bowl. The first meal he tried to eat in this way so disgusted his delicate stomach (used to the handiwork of a master chef) that he vomited. However, he was prepared to endure anything for an answer, a cure for the sufferings of life.

He apprenticed himself to two meditation teachers: Ārāda Kālāma and Udraka Rāmapūtra. Both taught him how to develop exalted states of consciousness through silent contemplation. So fiercely did his question burn inside him that Siddhārtha proved an able pupil. He soon attained the same high meditative states as his teachers. They both invited him to stay with them. The first teacher suggested that he co-lead his group, the second that he take over his group altogether.[1] However, Siddhārtha was not satisfied. The states he had attained through meditation were very blissful, but they had not resolved his question. He could sit happily absorbed in concentration for long periods but, when he emerged, death was still waiting to claim him. These masters taught the most advanced meditations of their day, and Siddhārtha found them wanting. He would have to try another approach.

There was no shortage of possibilities. It was a time of great ferment and experimentation in northern India. From about a hundred years beforehand, a kind of restlessness had seized its people. Thousands had found home life too cramping, and had begun wandering from place to place. The country was rich and prosperous, and could support this large floating population. Among them were exponents of many philosophies, and practitioners of all kinds of methods which they claimed led to truth. Some, such as Ajita of the Hair Blanket, were known far and wide. Some of the practices they advocated were quite extreme.

One possible way to truth which was held in high esteem was the path of asceticism. It was the body which was the culprit, held hostage by old age, sickness, and death. Deny the body, master it, and your spirit would be free. So ran the ascetic philosophy. People were prepared to torture themselves in this attempt to transcend themselves. Ascetics had been known to stand with an arm held upright in the air until it withered. They went naked in the cold. They starved themselves. One could not help but admire their determination, the fierce glint of battle in their sunken eyes. Siddhārtha was prepared to try.

He later said that nobody had ever gone further in practising austerities. He fasted till he was just bones, skin, and sinew. He could put his hands against his stomach and feel his backbone. He practised holding his breath to the point of breakdown. The catalogue of his asceticisms makes painful reading. In the midst of agony and exhaustion, when every nerve screamed for relief, he would remember his quest for a realm beyond birth and death, and crush down his resistance. So far did he take his austerities that he won an admiring audience. His fame rang like a great bell across northern India and disciples flocked to him.

However, at the height of his fame, and with a will forged into steel by self-denial, Siddhārtha still was not satisfied. He had pushed and striven and suffered. He had followed asceticism to the gates of death, yet still no answer had come. Old age, sickness, and death sat and wryly applauded him. He had not challenged them, in fact so racked was his body that he had put himself more firmly in their power than ever. Despite all the adulation he was receiving as a great ascetic it was time to give up, to try something else. He began to eat more, just a little boiled rice. That small bowl of food was enough to drive away his followers. They went off in disgust. The great ascetic had gone soft.

Siddhārtha was left alone, more alone than ever in his life. He had tried different ways supposed to lead to truth with total dedication, yet still no light had dawned. The darkness felt blacker than ever.

Out of the darkness came a memory. He was quite young, sitting outdoors, under a rose-apple tree. From its shade he was watching his father ploughing. Relaxed by the slow steady movements of the ox-team, and enjoying the coolness under the tree, he had gradually become deeply content, and his mind had become concentrated, lucid, and buoyant.

This memory may just have come to him as a compensation, a pleasurable experience to escape from his pain-racked state, or it may have been thrown up as Siddhārtha ransacked his past for some hint or clue to find a new approach to his quest. Whichever it was, he suddenly realized its significance.

In his early life everything had come easily to him. He had been relaxed to the point of slackness, lulled into dullness by pleasure. Then, after seeing through the surface glitter of the palace, he had left home and sought out not pleasure but pain. Both lifestyles had left him dissatisfied. In his palace he was always distracted. After his departure he had forced himself to concentrate, to bend his will to storm the gates of higher states of consciousness. Distraction and forced concentration had both played him false. Suppose he were to let go of pleasure and pain? Suppose he were to concentrate in an easy and relaxed way?

He walked alone, searching now not for a harsh environment for his austerities, nor for people, dancing, and laughter, but for a beautiful place in nature, like his rose-apple tree, which would calm his mind and provide helpful conditions in which to meditate steadily. He was still very weak, so he accepted some milk-rice from a woman called Sujātā. The effect, after his years of severe fasting, was to pour new life and energy into his emaciated frame.

He came to a peaceful place near the banks of the River Nerañjarā, found a tree with spreading branches, and sat down beneath it. Though he planned to meditate in a relaxed way, his determination was greater than ever. He was not going to leave that spot until he was Enlightened, or dead. It was May, the hottest month, and walking further wasn't easy. Anyway there was nowhere else to go. He had tried everything. This was his last throw.

He sat calmly under the spreading tree, enjoying the scene. Then he closed his eyes and allowed his mind to become still. Hours passed, and his stillness gradually deepened. Gently and steadily his concentration gathered momentum. His mind became a beacon of brilliant light. It was intensely pleasurable, but Siddhārtha knew not to cling to pleasure. He just allowed all the energies of his being to keep flowing together. As the process continued, he felt healed. No longer ground down by asceticism, he felt zestful. The beacon of his mind became so brilliant that it began to light up the past. He remembered his whole life, right back to his earliest childhood. Then he found he could recall his previous lives. As his concentration flowed on, he recalled endless past lives. Here he had been born, with this name, had lived in this way, died at that age, and been reborn in that place. On and on. There was no end to it.

As time passed, the details of these lives, which had seized his interest at first, began to pall. He was left with a pattern, an endless repetition. It was a rhythm of birth, growth, disease, and death. The rhythm never faltered; death's drummer never ceased. Birth and death, birth and death: it was like listening to suffering's heartbeat.

Still Siddhārtha allowed his concentrated mind to illuminate existence. The doors of his own continuum of existences had opened, now the walls which separated him from others began to fall away. He saw the lives of endless beings, saw their struggles, successes, and failures. He heard the unfailing rhythm running through their lives. Birth, death, and another birth.

Siddhārtha searched to understand the laws that governed this ceaseless flow of change. He began to notice a rising and falling pattern within the flux of rebirth. He saw how those beings who had based their lives on love, kindness, and generosity had been reborn in happy circumstances. Those who succumbed to hatred, jealousy, and greed inevitably found themselves in states of suffering. Watching life after life, he could predict the outcome of people's actions in their future rebirths. If you spread happiness, you received happiness; if you caused pain and separation, you found yourself alone in a hostile world. It was so clear. Yet beings were too caught up in their own concerns, their petty schemings, to see it.

Finally, seeing all of time and space laid out like a canvas before him, Siddhārtha identified step by step the process by which the endless rhythm of birth and death was set up. Birth and death were born from craving. It was the momentum of desire for existence which led beings on from life to life, lambs to the slaughter. With the ceasing of desire, birth and death died away. Siddhārtha lived out the process he was seeing. In the beacon of his vision, craving withered and died. The drumbeat was silent at last. As birth and death dissolved away, time and space vanished. All limitations whatsoever fell away. There was just light, total clarity, perfect understanding.

Siddhārtha, the limited human personality, had disappeared. He had awakened from the dream of suffering, of birth and death. There was just infinite freedom. When he opened his eyes, to see the morning star hovering in the eastern sky, he gazed at it with the total comprehension of a Buddha.

He spent several weeks at that place by the Nerañjarā. The impact of his realization was so strong that it took time to permeate his being. Also, he had a new question to resolve: was there any point in trying to communicate what he had seen? Through tremendous efforts he had managed to reverse the whole natural trend of his being. Instead of being carried along by craving and aversion he had moved against them, like a salmon leaping upstream. Most people were lost in craving, what would be the point of trying to change them? He would become frustrated and exhaust himself for nothing.

However, his vision of all beings suffering repeatedly because of craving had moved him to his depths. He could not abandon them. A great compassion for their sufferings welled up in his heart. He began wondering where to start. Eventually, his mind made up, he left the place of his Enlightenment, where he had prepared to die if need be, and walked towards Sarnath. Staying in the Deer Park at that time were five men who had been his closest companions when he had practised austerities. They had left him when he began to eat again, but he bore them no grudge for deserting him.

The five emaciated men saw Siddhārtha approaching them across the park. They looked at one another, doubtful. They weren't going to pay him any respect. He might once have been their leader and inspiration, but he had gone back to the life of luxury, eating rice pudding! They watched him approaching, mindful and serene, his face radiant from his experience beside the river. Despite themselves, they were soon on their feet to meet him and offer him a seat.

What followed is often described as the Buddha's 'first sermon', which is exactly what it was not. The Buddha knew these five men; they had been his friends and comrades-in-arms in the struggles of asceticism. Like all battle-hardened veterans of the ascetic life they were tough-minded and stubborn. They didn't go in for sermons; they needed straight talking. So what ensued was a very vigorous debate. The Buddha strove, with all the force of his freshly-Enlightened personality, to convince them that he had found the way to Truth. It was a middle way between hedonism and asceticism. It was a path of skilful actions leading to the 'deathless state'.

The debate continued for a long time. Some of the ascetics would leave for a while, to beg alms for the six of them, then return to the fray. The Buddha, tireless, just kept pushing home his message. His conviction and confidence were absolute. Listening to him talk was like hearing a lion roar.

Finally, one of the ascetics, whose name was Kauṇḍinya,[2] understood – and not just intellectually. The same vision of existence arose in his mind as the Buddha had seen under his tree. The Buddha recognized what had happened at once, and cried out 'Kauṇḍinya knows! Kauṇḍinya knows!' The Buddha's joy was boundless. He had wondered if anyone would be able to see the truth that he had discovered; now he was seeing that truth mirrored back to him in Kauṇḍinya's eyes. If Kauṇḍinya could understand then, in time, more people could understand; the whole world could understand. So the Buddha let out his cry of delight, and ever after Kauṇḍinya was known as 'Kauṇḍinya who knows'.

From that point, the Buddha's teaching, his beloved Dharma, spread like wildfire. One by one each of the five ascetics experienced the Truth. Next a young man called Yaśa, the son of a merchant at Sarnath, came to the Deer Park, and was soon convinced from his own experience of the truth of the Buddha's teaching. Yaśa had many friends in the town and surrounding countryside who then flocked to the Buddha. In no time at all there were sixty Enlightened beings in the world. Then the Buddha sent his disciples out to the world to teach 'the Dharma that is good in the beginning, good in the middle, and good in the end' for 'the welfare and happiness of many, out of compassion for the world'. So the sixty Enlightened disciples set off in different directions, wandering from place to place and teaching the Dharma.

In this way, the Buddha began his work of communicating the way to Enlightenment, to which he was to devote the remaining years of his long life, with unremitting zeal and energy. He himself spent most of the year wandering in northern India, begging his food, meditating, and teaching. He taught all manner of people: from royalty to lepers. During the monsoon rains he would remain in one place, often in the vicinity of some large city, and continue teaching.

He also paid visits to the Śākyans. Śuddhodana his father, and Mahāprajāpati his aunt, both gained Enlightenment under his instruction. His son Rāhula and some of his cousins left their homes and 'went forth' as *bhikshus*, or monks (though the word 'monk' has rather different connotations). According to tradition, Rāhula gained Enlightenment at the age of twenty. The Buddha's cousin, Ānanda, became the devoted attendant of his later years. Ānanda was gifted with a prodigious memory, and according to tradition it is his accounts of the Buddha's teaching and incidents in his life which are preserved in the *suttas* (or discourses) of the Pali canon and the *sūtras* of the Mahāyāna.

By the time the Buddha was old, his followers numbered many thousands. This was not without its problems. In particular, another of the Buddha's cousins, Devadatta, tried to provoke a schism among his disciples, and even made unsuccessful attempts on the Buddha's life. To his dying day the Buddha displayed complete mental sharpness and awareness, compassion, fearlessness, patience, and a wisdom that he could express in as many ways as there were people.

Finally, at the age of eighty, he made one last long tour, moving painfully from place to place. His body had done enough. He could only avoid its aches and pains by withdrawing into deep meditation. Yet the pain never ruffled his mental equanimity; he just let it be. Touring with Ānanda, he visited nearly all the main centres of his teaching.

At last, unable to go further, he came to a grove of sāl trees near a village called Kuśinagara, in the country of the Mallians. There he lay down on his right side, in what is known as the 'lion posture'. Even at the point of death, however, he was completely aware, and only concerned for others. A wanderer called Subhadra who had come to see him was turned away by Ānanda, who did not want the Buddha troubled on his deathbed. But the Buddha insisted on talking with him, and Subhadra, convinced of the Dharma, became his last personal disciple. The Buddha also comforted Ānanda who, not reconciled to the fact that even Buddhas must die, was deeply upset.

Finally the Buddha addressed all the disciples who had assembled there. With his last breaths he asked if any of them had any unresolved doubts or questions about the Dharma which he could settle before he passed away. With typical thoughtfulness, he suggested that anyone who was embarrassed to ask directly could do so through a friend. Still the assembly was silent. By speech and supreme example the Buddha had made the Dharma unmistakably clear.

Seeing that the whole assembly had no doubts, the Buddha gave his final advice and exhortation: 'All compounded things are impermanent, with mindfulness strive on!' Then he passed into deep meditation and died. His mind had long been perfectly controlled and joyful. In sloughing off his body he was freed of his only remaining source of suffering and limitation, and entered the bliss of total liberation.

The Buddha died as he had lived, inspiring others to practise the Dharma and to arrive at total happiness. Since setting rolling 'the Wheel of the Dharma', as it is known, in the Deer Park at Sarnath, he had never tired of turning it. That great wheel rolled on after his death, throughout most of Asia. It has rolled down the centuries, inspiring millions of people. Now it has rolled into the West, into our busy twenty-first century lives. Ancient India may seem very distant in time and culture from our world of traffic jams and busy airports. But the essential features of the Buddha's odyssey in search of an end to the fears of illness, old age, and death – what I have called the 'central myth' of Buddhism – can speak to us as directly as it did to people 2,500 years ago.

Śākyamuni Buddha

Two

The Development of
Buddhist Visualization

In the previous chapter we went back 2,500 years to meet with Śākya-muni Buddha in ancient India. However, there is a way in which we can encounter an Enlightened One which does not involve travelling in time and space. According to Buddhism, we can meet a Buddha in the 'universe within', by leaving behind the world of the senses through meditation. If we are highly developed spiritually this can even happen spontaneously in dreams and visions. But the most common method of contacting a Buddha is through deep concentration on the visualized image of a particular Buddha figure.

All the figures we shall meet in this book can be meditated upon using visualization *sādhanas* – set methods of spiritual practice. Before we go any further we shall explore one of these sādhanas. The meditation we shall look at is a very simple visualization of the Buddha at the time of his Enlightenment. Over the centuries, many sādhanas of Śākyamuni have developed. They focus on different aspects of his activity. For example, one form of visualization involves seeing the Buddha teaching, seated on a great throne supported by lions – symbolizing the total confidence of his 'lion's roar' of the Truth.

A visualization sādhana of Śākyamuni Buddha

The meditation begins, as do nearly all visualizations, with the appearance of blue sky. We sit quietly, allowing our minds to become calm, gently trying to let the concerns of the everyday world drop away. In imagination we allow everything to dissolve into a vast expanse of blue sky, stretching away into the distance. This blue sky symbolizes *śūnyatā*, the true nature of everything, of which all forms are just temporary expressions. It is the stainless nature of the mind, reflecting forms but unsullied and unaffected by them.

After dwelling in this calm blueness for a while, a flat, grassy plain appears in front of us. In the far distance are snow-capped mountain peaks. We feel the expansiveness of the plain, see the bright colours of the grass. Next, in the foreground, sprouts a spreading bodhi tree – a 'tree of awakening'. It has a silver trunk, wide-reaching branches, and heart-shaped dark green leaves. Under the tree is a mound of a kind of grass, known as *kuśa*, piled up to form a seat. On the seat is a pure white cloth.

So far, the scene we have been building up in our imagination is a quite natural one. It is a realistic representation of the scene at Bodh Gaya – except that with a little poetic licence the snow-capped Himalayas have come into view on the northern horizon. From now on, however, we begin to enter a different world.

On the white cloth appears a golden lotus seat. Seated on the golden lotus is Śākyamuni Buddha, cross-legged in meditation. His body is made of golden light, shining brilliantly. He wears the saffron robes of a monk, with one shoulder uncovered. His hands rest in his lap in the meditation position, one on top of the other, supporting a large black begging-bowl. His hair is blue-black and curly. He is smiling serenely, his eyes half closed. His figure is surrounded by an aura of golden light, and gives off a feeling of deep peacefulness and infinite compassion. At the centre of his chest is a radiant golden *dharmacakra* – a wheel (usually with eight spokes, symbolizing the Buddha's teaching of the Eightfold Path) which is a symbol of the Dharma.

We have now built up the full visualization of Śākyamuni Buddha, blazing with light. This in itself can have an uplifting effect on the mind. However, in sādhanas, building up the visualized figure is only the first movement in a symphony of form, colour, and sound. A sādhana plays out in vivid forms before the mind's eye the whole drama of following the spiritual path. In a sense, so far, we have sat back and watched the visualization develop. It is now time to start interacting with it.

Next, then, a ray of golden light comes from the heart of the Buddha, and gently penetrates our own heart. ('Heart' here means 'heart centre' – the core of your being inside the centre of the chest, not the physical pumping mechanism). Down this ray of light stream golden letters. We read them as they pour into our hearts. They make up the words: *oṃ muni muni mahāmuni śākyamuni svāhā*. This is one version of the mantra of Śākyamuni. While continuing to see the golden figure in front of us, we are now going to add a vocal or aural dimension to the experience. *Muni* means silent one or sage. *Mahā* means great. *Śākyamuni* – the sage of the Śākyas – is a common epithet of Siddhārtha Gautama, the Buddha of our age. In receiving the mantra from his heart, we are receiving the Dharma. Since we are now inhabiting the archetypal level, that Dharma comes not in the form of a rational discourse, but in its symbolic essence. Contained within these fifteen syllables is the concentrated wisdom and compassion of the Buddha.

We now recite the mantra, first aloud, and then silently to ourselves. As we do so, we feel that the Buddha's wisdom, compassion, and purity have entered into us, and we have been transformed from the unenlightened to the Enlightened state. We can recite the mantra for as long as we wish, though traditionally this is done in multiples of 108, a *mālā* (Buddhist rosary) being used to keep count.

After the mantra recitation we just sit quietly. We move from activity to receptivity. We try simply to be aware, so that we can experience the change in our consciousness wrought by the visualization and mantra recitation. In this way we allow our spiritual intuition full play to absorb the 'Dharma-message' that the practice communicates.

Finally, we allow the visualization to fade away. We dissolve it in reverse order to that in which we built it up, until we are once more seeing just the vast expanse of the sky. When we are ready, we let the blue sky fade away as well. The visualization is complete. It only remains for us to dedicate the 'merits' or beneficial effects of the practice, for the welfare and Enlightenment of all beings. These practices are always set squarely in a Mahāyāna context of universal compassion. In performing the sādhana we are using a very effective method to further our own development, but we see that our spiritual growth is intricately linked with that of all living beings. We visualize the Buddha so that we may become a Buddha, because having become an embodiment of total wisdom and compassion we shall be able in our turn to revolve the wheel of the Dharma and put paid to suffering in the world.

Three modes of experiencing a Buddha

We have now encountered the Buddha in two ways. Firstly we saw his life in ancient India: leaving home, practising austerities, gaining Enlightenment under the bodhi tree, teaching the Dharma and gathering a large following, before finally passing away at the age of eighty. Then in visualization we encountered him in a resplendent archetypal form and experienced the Dharma taught through light, colour, form, and mantric sound. We now need to examine the relationship between these two experiences. This will help us to understand more of the nature of Buddhahood and of the different figures we shall be meeting in this book. To start with we shall look at a story which should help to clarify the different ways in which one can experience a Buddha.

Suppose that in ancient India a young merchant meets the Buddha. He is impressed by him and invites him to eat at his house, along with his accompanying monks. While he busies himself waiting personally on the Buddha, he has a chance to observe him. At the time of the meeting the Buddha is sixty years old, say. So the merchant sees a man of stately bearing and refined manners (the Buddha was, after all, the son of a ruler). He is tall with dark hair, perhaps sprinkled with grey. His face is lined and weather-beaten as he has spent most of his life outdoors under the Indian sun. He moves slowly and gracefully, and gives total attention to what he is doing. He radiates kindness and care for those around him, and yet at the same time that he is seated in his dining room, the merchant feels that the Buddha is in contact with other levels, other dimensions of being. He is a strange conundrum – the most approachable of all humanity, yet somehow set apart from the worries of the world. Even after the Buddha has taken up his begging-bowl and departed, a feeling of calm yet vibrant energy hangs in the dining hall.

The son and daughter of the merchant are both quite young at the time that the Buddha comes to eat. They cannot understand the discourse he gives after finishing his meal – something about form, feelings, recognition, volitions, and consciousness all being devoid of any fixed unchanging self. They just remember his presence. It is as though a world-ruler or a *deva*, an angelic being, had come to visit their house! They never forget that day, and when they are older they both tell their father that they want to leave home to practise the Dharma – the Buddha's teaching – full-time.

The merchant is distraught at first. Who will look after his expanding business if his beloved son doesn't take it over? And his pretty dark-eyed daughter plans to cut off her long black hair and wander unprotected from place to place. What will become of her? And no grandchildren! And yet, and yet, the Buddha was right, all compounded things are impermanent, and to cling to them causes only suffering. So he gives his blessing, sad, anxious, and yet hopeful that his children may find a freedom greater than he has managed to discover in life.

Son and daughter join the Buddha's monastic followers. The young man passes most of the year wandering from place to place, but he spends as much time as possible meditating, under shady trees or in rough shelters. After he has been living in this way for seven or eight years he hears a dreadful piece of news. The Buddha has passed away! All the monks in the area assemble to hear the monk who has brought the message. He explains that the Buddha did not die at Śrāvastī or Sarnath, or any great city. He passed away near a little village called Kuśinagara, lying in a grove of sāl trees. The messenger carefully repeats the details of the scene: the Buddha lying on his right side, giving his assembled followers his final exhortation: 'With mindfulness, strive on!'

The merchant's son grieves that he will never see the Buddha again. At the same time, he is fired by the account of the Buddha's calm death, and his last words. He sits under a tree, and establishes his concentration. Then he pictures the Buddha as he knew him: walking, teaching, sitting in meditation. Filled with gratitude and loving memories, he slips gradually into a state of deep meditation.

As he does so, still absorbed in his images of the Buddha, a change takes place. Some of his memories had been of the Buddha as he had last seen him – old and infirm, making wry comments about his body being like a rickety wagon held together with bits of rope. However, in the depths of his meditation, his memories are transformed. The Buddha appears radiant, vigorous. It is as though the physical details had dropped away, leaving just the essence, as though he were looking at the Buddha's Enlightened personality expressed in colour and form. As he becomes even more absorbed in meditation, the Buddha's figure becomes brighter. It seems to be giving off a golden light. Somehow, too, the radiance is not just light, it is charged with all the qualities of compassion, alertness, and spiritual power which he first sensed as a young boy playing in his father's dining hall.

The image becomes so overwhelming, so total, that he has no sense of it being his memory. It is as though his memories were the gateway through which something else had entered in. This shining Buddha does not feel as though it is his mental creation. It *is* the Buddha, more real than when he ever saw him in 'real life'.

After a time, which to him seems timeless, the experience begins to fade. The light becomes dimmer, everyday thoughts begin to insinuate themselves into the cracks in his concentration. Eventually he is back with his body, stretching cramped limbs and noticing mosquito bites. However, he no longer grieves for the Buddha. The wagon may finally have fallen to pieces and been burned, but after this experience he will never think of the Buddha as 'dead and gone'.

Twenty years later, the merchant is organizing another meal in his dining hall. The room has become much more sumptuously decorated. Business is better than ever. However, he takes little delight in the splendours he has accumulated. He has aged greatly these last few years. First his wife dying, and then the news that his son had died of a fever!

He swaps memories with the female wanderer who is his chief guest. She is very thin now, and her dark eyes burn with a fathomless light. He is almost scared of this changeling daughter. She is completely unruffled by the family deaths. It seems unnatural. He reproaches her, saying that she has become hard and selfish. 'Don't you miss your own mother and brother?' 'No,' comes the gentle answer, 'in meditation one day I glimpsed how all things arise and pass away, like clouds forming and fading back into the sky. It wasn't just an idea, father, it was a direct experience. I knew then that I had seen the Dharma for myself. So I will not grieve for passing clouds, though I feel grateful that they appeared in the sky for a little while.' When she is gone, the merchant feels, as he did once before, a calm, vibrant energy remains in his dining hall.

This story presents us with three types of experience of the Buddha. In the first, the merchant sees the Buddha sitting in his dining hall. Years later, his son sees the Buddha moving about with difficulty, his mind still totally alert, but expressing itself through an ageing body. So they both see the physical form of the Buddha, located in space and time, in northern India. This experience of the Buddha is known as his *nirmāṇakāya*, his 'body of form' or 'created body'. Later, after hearing of the Buddha's passing away, the young monk sits down and concentrates on his memories of the Buddha. These, too, are mental representations of the Buddha as he actually appeared physically. They are mental images of the *nirmāṇakāya* form.

Then, however, something happens. Through the power of his devotion, his concentration deepens. His consciousness 'rises', becomes clearer, more radiant. He enters into a meditative absorption, known technically as *dhyāna*. In this superconscious state, his mental image of the Buddha changes, as though he had risen above the clouds and seen the sun unveiled. In this heightened inner experience the Buddha becomes a resplendent, archetypal being. At this level of consciousness his figure becomes refined – a play of light and colour, and the experience of his Enlightened qualities is direct and intuitive. This archetypal form is known as the *sambhogakāya* – the 'glorious body' or 'body of mutual enjoyment'. At this level, the experience of separation, of a boundary between oneself as meditating subject and the Buddha as the concentration object, has melted and softened to a large degree.

Finally, we may gather from the daughter's reply to her father's reproach that she has gone a stage further still. Some degree of insight into the real nature of things has arisen within her. She has had a direct intuitive experience of the Enlightened state. It is as if the boundary between the Buddha and her has not just softened, it has dissolved away altogether, and she sees the world through the Buddha's eyes. She directly experiences the truth of the Dharma – unmediated by words, images, or even symbols. This experience of Reality, a direct perception of Buddhahood, is called the *dharmakāya*, or 'truth body', of a Buddha.

This distinction of the three *kāyas* of a Buddha should give us a fuller picture of Buddhahood. A Buddha is, essentially, a totally unconditioned consciousness, beyond time and space, the *dharmakāya*. However, for the purposes of communicating the way to Enlightenment, he appears both on the archetypal plane, as a radiant *sambhogakāya* form, and in the material world, the world of the senses, as a *nirmāṇakāya*.

How we experience a Buddha depends on our level of consciousness. If we live in the sense-realm, which is a 'fragmented' state of awareness, then we shall see the *nirmāṇakāya* – just the physical form. If we are capable of focusing our awareness more, and rising into higher states of consciousness through meditation, then we can experience the blissful, refined *sambhogakāya*. Finally, if we can produce the concentration and clarity to penetrate into the true nature of things, we shall become Enlightened. At this level, we and the Buddha will not be separate, and we shall experience all phenomena as reflections of the *dharmakāya*.

The sources of Śākyamuni visualization

Visualization seems to have been practised by the Buddha's early disciples in two forms. Firstly there was *kasiṇa* meditation. Kasiṇas are objects of concentration which are still used today to produce entry into higher states of consciousness. For example, coloured discs can be employed. If we were going to practise kasiṇa meditation we should first obtain, say, a large bunch of red flowers, and arrange them into a disc on the ground. Then we should sit, with eyes open, concentrating on the disc. We would continue meditating in this way until we were capable of holding the image in our minds with our eyes closed. At this stage we would see a mental image of the disc of flowers with their stems, leaves, and so on. Finally, through deepening our concentration on the mental image, we might begin to enter a higher state of consciousness. At that point, the physical details of the image would fall away, and we should find ourselves dwelling in delightful concentration on a shining disc of pure red light. The Pali suttas give a list of ten kinds of kasiṇa, and the Theravāda commentator Buddhaghosa gives an extensive commentary on their use.[3]

The other main form of visualization in early Buddhism seems to have been 'Recollection of the Buddha'. The Pali texts explain this form of meditation as a rational one, recalling the qualities of a Buddha, perhaps using a stock phrase, such as, 'This Blessed One is holy, a fully Enlightened One, perfected in wisdom and conduct, faring happily, knower of the worlds, unsurpassed leader of men to be trained, teacher of heavenly beings and men, a Buddha, a Blessed One.'[4]

However, it seems inconceivable that early disciples of the Buddha should not have embellished this to include an imaginative reconstruction of events in the Buddha's life. The Buddha had recommended that the sites of his birth, Enlightenment, first teaching, and *parinirvāṇa* (or passing away) should become places of pilgrimage. Many of his followers must have made daily pilgrimages to these places in their mind's eye – seeing the Buddha meditating, teaching, and mindfully walking from place to place. Through intense and devoted concentration on the Buddha's *nirmāṇakāya*,[5] higher states of consciousness would have dawned, just as they did in the case of the merchant's son. In the clearer, more rarefied, air of these dhyāna states, the Buddha's body would have become more radiant until it became a *sambhogakāya* form, 'blazing with signs and marks'.

We know that, after the Buddha's passing away, many of his disciples worked at ways of achieving visions of him. The *avadānas*, which tell the stories of the Buddha's closest disciples, describe visionary experiences which are quite similar to the visualizations described in sādhanas. Descriptions of these meditative visions would then be given to less accomplished meditators. Using the description of the characteristics of the *sambhogakāya* form as their starting point for meditation, it was easier for them to enter the higher states in which they were spontaneously experienced. Certain of these descriptions became well known, even standard, so various 'visualization sādhanas' developed that could be passed from one generation of meditators to the next.

If we combine these traditions of kasiṇa meditation and recollection of the Buddha, we arrive at the basic elements of the visualization sādhanas of Buddhas which are practised today. The two streams flow together into a uniquely satisfying whole. From kasiṇas come the colour, light, and deep concentration on a static object. From recollection of the Buddha we add devotion, emotional richness, movement, and contemplation of the qualities of an Enlightened being.

The appearance of new figures

By now it should be clear how sādhanas of Śākyamuni Buddha have come about. But if you have looked into Buddhist iconography you will have come across scores of other figures, some of whom seem far removed in appearance from the peaceful Buddha seated beneath his tree with his robe and bowl. Where did all these other figures appear from?

The simple answer is that they arose from the depths of the minds of experienced meditators, people who had gained spiritual experience through years of practice. Usually they began by practising one or more traditional sādhanas for many years, carefully following the text of the meditation in which everything would be laid down: the form of the figures to be visualized, their positions and gestures, colours, and so on. Faithfully practising in this way over many years, they came to experience the visualized form as a pointer to an experience which goes beyond form. Once they had arrived at the spiritual 'point' – to receive the message that the practice was communicating – they no longer needed the form. Having glimpsed Reality shining beyond all forms, they were free to allow it to express itself in new or varied guises. If those new figures proved helpful to other people as pointers in the direction of Reality, a new visualization tradition would emerge.

This does not mean that a yogin or yogini who has arrived at deep spiritual understanding 'thinks up' new forms. It is more as though appropriate forms appear to them. They perceive them through their spiritual intuition. As we noted earlier, this may happen in dreams and visions as well as in formal meditation.

If we look at the process historically, we see that the tapestry of visualization practice became much richer with the development of the Mahāyāna – the 'great way'. Far more Buddha forms began to appear, and the historical Buddha, Śākyamuni, became one among many. Also, the Bodhisattvas, the crown princes and princesses of Buddhism – beings who have vowed to aid all sentient beings to gain Enlightenment – began to manifest, dressed in jewels and silks. Many Mahāyāna sūtras are visualizations in themselves if you allow your imagination to come to life as you read them. They also sometimes describe scenes designed for formal visualization meditation – such as the series of fourteen meditations given in the *Amitāyur Dhyāna Sūtra*. These begin with meditation on the red disc of the setting sun (a kasiṇa meditation in a different context), and build up into a vast visualization of the Buddha Amitāyus ('Infinite Life'), his attendants, and all the splendours of his world, Sukhāvatī.

In Tantric Buddhism, also known as the Vajrayāna ('way of the diamond thunderbolt'), visualization ran riot – one might say. Meditations proliferated like jungle plants. Many new elements entered: Tantric initiation as a necessary preliminary to practice, the introduction of magical rituals as the basic structure for some visualizations, visualizing *yourself* as the Buddha or Bodhisattva rather than just seeing the figure in front of you, the addition of other types of figure to visualize, such as gurus, yidams, ḍākinīs, and dharmapālas. One of the great contributions of the Tantra to Buddhism is the realization that Reality can be communicated through many forms other than peaceful and attractive Buddhas and Bodhisattvas. In the course of centuries the Tantra has 'converted' the darkest denizens of the unconscious – the powerful and terrifying, the seductive, the wild – and shown that Reality can express itself through any of them. (We shall meet these 'dark armies of the Dharma' in the third book of this series.) With tremendous creative energy the Vajrayāna greatly expanded the scope of visualization. The Tantric universe is still expanding, with new sādhanas being composed to the present day.

The development of new sādhanas

Buddhism's exploration of the archetypal realm has now continued for more than two millennia. As well as revealing new figures, this process has also produced a steady stream of fresh sādhanas centring on figures whose forms have not changed for over a thousand years. For example, in the next book of this series we shall meet Green Tārā, an embodiment of transcendental compassion, a figure quite familiar to the Buddhists of tenth century India. Over the centuries, many new sādhanas associated with her have been produced, until the number of her visualizations must now total many hundreds.

New sādhanas are sometimes created out of inner compulsion, in the same way that some books and pieces of music are written. There is a driving force within the mind of the meditator that demands expression in a new form. However, many sādhanas are composed by Buddhist teachers to answer the needs of their pupils for sādhanas of particular types. For example, someone may not have time to perform a lengthy one, so after careful consideration their guru may write an abbreviated version, condensing all the main points of the original. Someone else may be very devotional by nature, and the guru may write for them a sādhana of a particular figure that involves a great deal of making of offerings. Most such sādhanas do not incorporate new elements, they are variations on standard 'recipes', recombining well-known ingredients. Thus, although there are many thousands of sādhanas, certain procedures recur in nearly all of them. This will be noticeable as we describe some sādhanas in the following chapters.

Three

The Benefits of Visualization

Buddhist practice is not a spectator sport. Some acts of great heroism, generosity, energy, and self-sacrifice may be performed in public, and it is relatively easy to divine the states of mind that motivated them. However, spiritual development being essentially an inner working on the mind, it may find little obvious external expression. If you had sat by the River Nerañjarā and watched the Buddha gain Enlightenment, what would you have seen? Unless you were spiritually sensitive, you would have witnessed an emaciated man with a determined expression sit down under a tree. He would have closed his eyes in meditation, and then sat unmoving day and night. Eventually, if you had not become bored and wandered off, you would have seen him get up, smiling radiantly, and pace up and down. He would then have spent several weeks doing nothing much, until finally he strode off in the direction of the city of Sarnath. Unless you understood and were moved by the spiritual significance of what was happening, you would probably have found a tortoise marathon more compelling.

Because spiritual transformation can be hard to perceive from the outside, visualization attempts to take us 'inside' the Buddha's experience. The elements of the practices show us the world as seen by an Enlightened mind. Visualization is visionary experience re-enacted. A Buddha experiences a transformed world of light and colour, the play of Reality. Through visualization we put ourselves into such a world and, by doing so, little by little we make it our natural mode of seeing. When we can continuously experience the world as a Buddha does, then we shall have become a Buddha.

Visualization gives us a taste of the spiritual life in a way that words never can. We may talk about a Bodhisattva developing the fullness of compassion, and appreciate the meaning of the words. However, as we saw in the Introduction, in visualization we can come face to face with a Buddha or Bodhisattva whose smile radiates compassion to the universe, and whose gentle eyes melt with love for all living beings. In visualization we do not just hear about the Dharma, we live it out. It is this imaginative participation in higher spiritual experience that makes visualization such an effective tool for self-transformation.

Entering, in imagination, into the world as perceived by an Enlightened being has many benefits. Here we shall concentrate on exploring how a visualization can help us develop understanding of the real nature of things, and how it can involve and refine our emotions.

Developing wisdom through visualization – emptiness of inherent existence

Buddhism makes a distinction in the field of meditation between practices with different aims. In particular, it divides meditation into *śamatha* and *vipaśyanā* practices. *Śamatha* means calm. Meditations of this type aim to calm and concentrate the mind. They give access to the higher states of consciousness termed *dhyāna* (Sanskrit, *jhāna* in Pali), which are characterized by contentment and one-pointedness of mind. Using them as a basis, one can then develop *vipaśyanā*, or insight into Reality. This insight is crucial, since having experienced it you arrive at an unshakeable faith in the Dharma, and your eventual attainment of Enlightenment is assured. If you develop only śamatha, then however blissful your mental state, however focused your mind, you can still lose everything you have gained, and fall right back into the swamps of negative mental states. Śamatha is important because it makes the mind concentrated and flexible, a wieldy tool for developing insight. However, the changes it brings about are only temporary. Vipaśyanā 'imprints' the Dharma on your psyche in such a way that a permanent transformation is brought about.

Visualization combines elements of both śamatha and vipaśyanā. It can induce strong śamatha through contemplation of shining unmoving symbols and figures, or through the repetition of mantras. It also tries in a variety of ways to induce the vipaśyanā experience. The whole sādhana, everything that happens during its practice, is a dramatic portrayal of the nature of Reality. Through symbols and images the sādhana enables us to 'live through' the principles on which the universe is constructed.

Nearly all visualizations begin by asking us to see in our mind's eye a vast expanse of blue sky, absolutely clear, stretching away endlessly in all directions. Visualized day after day, this begins to convey various messages. On the simplest level, it encourages us to enter fully into the meditative state. In the blue sky all our worries and problems, likes and dislikes, have faded away. There is nothing to threaten or bother us. The sky is calm and bright, peaceful and expansive; by visualizing it our mind takes on the same characteristics. There is a tremendous freedom in this blue sky. We could fly through it forever, like an eagle, completely unobstructed. In all this, the blue sky is whispering its message to our spiritual intuition: the mind, in its essential nature, is like blue sky – vast, free, serene, and unobstructed.

The blue sky, as we saw, is a symbol for śūnyatā – 'emptiness' or 'voidness' – one of the most important terms in the whole of Buddhism. Insight into Reality is insight into śūnyatā, for śūnyatā is the ultimate nature of all things. All conditioned things are 'empty' or 'void' of any kind of fixed, unchanging essence. They are sky-like and ungraspable, like clouds. We may apply fixed concepts to them for practical purposes, for example, 'I am John. That is my house.' But ultimately, Reality defies our concepts and refuses to be limited by them. We cannot apply concepts to Reality, just as we cannot stick labels onto a flowing stream, or onto the sky. The universe is a dance, in ceaseless motion. Things arise out of Emptiness, given the right conditions, and when those conditions cease they disappear back into Emptiness. This day, this moment, this breath, see how they fly!

It is because the essential nature of everything is empty, śūnyatā, a 'no-nature', that everything can change, transform, and develop. If nothing is fixed, then anything can transform itself into anything. (Given time, perhaps, a frog can become a prince, or a prince a frog....) It also means that through conscious redirection of the flow of change in a positive way, we can transform every aspect of ourselves to gain Enlightenment.

Illustrating the dance of form and Emptiness, the blue sky begins to give birth to visions. In the Śākyamuni sādhana of the previous chapter we saw the grassy Indian plain appear from the sky, then the distant mountains, the bodhi tree, the seat, and finally the the shining golden Buddha, his body made of light.

Everything that appears in a visualization reminds us of wisdom because it is a symbol of the Dharma. If we visualize a Buddha, for example, each aspect of his figure has symbolic significance. We saw how the golden wheel on Śākyamuni's chest was a symbol for the Eightfold Path. In the same way, his colour, hand gesture, begging-bowl, and facial expression all have associations with a spiritual quality or an aspect of the Dharma. Every part of the figure functions to remind us of Reality, and points us towards Enlightenment.

From the Buddha's lustrous form, a ray of light came forth, down which the mantra travelled to enter our hearts. Mantras are sound-symbols. They consist of strings of syllables, often with no intelligible meaning. One popular etymology of the word '*mantra*' is that it derives from a Sanskrit root meaning 'to protect the mind'. Repetition of mantras strengthens our link with a particular embodiment of Enlightenment, or with some aspect of the Dharma. If we become concentrated during mantra-recitation, then our conceptualizations (which reinforce our sense of living in a world of fixed entities) die away, setting up the conditions for our minds to intuitively experience the true nature of things.

Finally, the whole phantasmagoria began to fade away. First the Buddha's body dissolved, then his seat, and so on, until all the evanescent forms had disappeared. Everything, even the shining colours and forms of the archetypal world of the visualization, was of the nature of the blue sky. The dissolution of the visualization reminds us that everything is impermanent; even shining Buddhas pass away. All that we experience, the heavens and hells that we create for ourselves and lock ourselves into by calling them 'real', are insubstantial. They are cloud-visions, arising in the blue sky of the mind. Seeing their empty, changing nature we can let them go, and experience the boundless freedom of our own true, unlimited nature.

Developing wisdom through visualization – non-duality

People who are fairly new to Buddhism, when they learn about visualizations of archetypal Buddhas, are often puzzled by a question: are these Buddhas external to us, or are they products of our own minds? To take the story from the previous chapter as an example, when the merchant saw the Buddha seated in his dining hall, the Buddha was clearly a separate person, part of the 'outer world'. But when the merchant's son saw the radiant image of the Buddha in his meditation, was he simply experiencing an aspect of his own consciousness, or was he making contact with a force, energy, or presence – call it what you will – that was external to him?

One way in which Buddhism answers these problems is by denying the terms in which the questions are put. Part of the Enlightened vision consists of an experience of non-duality. When you see Reality, you recognize that 'subject' and 'object' are just concepts which you impose on your experience. The barricades come down, and you can make only provisional distinctions between self and other, me and you, inside and outside. From the point of view of ultimate Reality, then, our questions have no meaning.

It is as though we were to take a piece of country, say Alsace-Lorraine in north-eastern France. At the moment we call these regions France, and say they are not part of Germany. Historians will tell you that between 1871 and 1919, and again during the Second World War, they were part of Germany, not part of France. Intellectually we draw our boundaries now here, now there. However, the hills and woods of those provinces know nothing of these distinctions. In themselves they are not 'German hills' or 'French trees'. In the same way we busily draw lines on our maps of consciousness: 'this is mine', 'that is nothing to do with me'. In reality, though, existence is seamless, and knows nothing of our mentally-imposed boundaries.

The sādhanas speak to us not only of impermanence and śūnyatā, they also help us to experience non-duality. During visualization practice we see shining, delicate forms made of pure light appear in front of us. These objects of our consciousness are so much more subtle than our usual objects of awareness that our sense of being faced with an objective world is refined. Because our sense of external objects and our sense of ourselves as subjects are just two aspects of the same experience, with the softening of the objects our sense of self also becomes subtler.

In some visualizations we refine our sense of self directly, by becoming a Buddha in imagination. Our physical body dissolves away into the blue sky, and in its place appears a light-body, appearing in the blueness as though carved from a rainbow. In these practices we are often asked to become a radiant figure gazing at other subtle forms which are then absorbed into us. In this way we imaginatively experience the merging of subject and object.

Nonetheless, even if we visualize the union of subject and object in meditation, then, assuming we are not Enlightened, when we emerge from the visualization we shall find ourselves back in a world that presents itself to us as dualistic. Moreover, in order to function in the everyday world we have to use language, which is inherently dualistic. So we have no choice. In trying to conceptualize about the status of the Buddhas, we can only think in terms of subject and object. The important point to recognize is that our decisions to regard the Buddha as internal or external are provisional. They are strategies for approaching the Truth rather than Truth itself.

Supposing we adopt the strategy of seeing 'the Buddha within', what consequences follow? On the positive side, it means that we have the potential to gain Buddhahood. It is latent within our consciousness, waiting for us to discover it. We have only to put effort into meditation and we shall contact our own Buddha nature. From this perspective, the different Enlightened figures of the Buddhist tradition exemplify qualities that we ourselves can develop. They become symbols of the peace, wisdom, compassion, and other positive qualities which will unfold as we progress on the Buddhist path. On the negative side, there is a danger that we may reduce the Buddhas to mere psychology. If the Buddhas are within us, products of our own consciousness, then we must be 'bigger' than them. Hence we diminish their importance. It is probably harder to feel devotion, to begin with at least, for something you think of as an aspect of your mind.

So if we see the Buddhas as aspects of our own mind, we feel Buddhahood as something attainable, but we may diminish it in stature. If we consider them to be outside, then the reverse tends to be true. When we contact Buddhas – in meditation, or by performing devotional practices – there is no particular danger of seeing them as being less than totally Enlightened, solvers of the riddles of existence. The problem is that as they are so fine and exalted, and external to us, that we may feel an unbridgeable gulf between us and them. In the same way as the average Christian worships God, but could not conceive of becoming God, so we may be content to worship the Buddhas from afar without developing any real confidence that we can *become* a Buddha. Yet the essence of Buddhism is that any human being who makes the effort can attain what the Buddha attained.

Buddhism, and especially the Buddhist Tantra, recognizing that neither of these strategies is ultimately true, is happy to adopt either of them as appropriate. Sometimes, you may be encouraged to devote yourself to a Buddha in meditation as though he were something completely beyond you; at other times to see him as a mirror of your own potential. Thus in Tantric meditation you will sometimes visualize a Buddha figure in front of you, and at other times you may see yourself becoming that Buddha. Once you have escaped from the trap of seeing a Buddha exclusively in terms of 'inside' or 'outside', you are free to adopt whatever attitude is most helpful. So in these pages we shall move freely from one mode to the other. Sometimes Buddhas will appear as forces at large in the universe, sometimes as symbols of our own potential.

Involving the emotions through visualization

We saw in the Introduction that it is impossible to make much spiritual progress on the basis of simple rational conviction. It is crucial that our emotions should be fully engaged with our Dharma practice. Visualization is extremely helpful in achieving this, as it is enjoyable and emotionally satisfying. In embarking on the meditation we enter a realm of light and colour that in itself stimulates warm feelings within us. More than this, though, visualization involves a personal relationship. Imagine that we meet a Buddha or Bodhisattva in our meditation for day after day. At first the figure is unclear, distant. Then, as we persevere, and perhaps our capacity to visualize improves, we begin to enjoy the company of this shining figure. It is a joy to see them. We look forward to our daily meetings. We feel bathed in their love and compassion, enriched by the brilliant rays of light which pour from their body into ours. We start to notice changes in ourselves as a result of our regular encounters with them. Something of their qualities begins to 'rub off' on us. Meeting them is like spending time with a good friend of overwhelming generosity and wisdom. Over a period of time, we may even gradually come to love them. They become the centre of our emotional world. Just by thinking about them outside meditation, something in us begins to glow.

To someone who has never performed such practices, what I have just described may sound like a recipe for madness. Are we not simply becoming lost in a fantasy world, giving a dream power over us? But the practitioner of visualization does not lose touch with the everyday world. He or she can distinguish the inner world from the domain of 'public reality', and does not confuse the experience of meditation with that of ordinary waking consciousness. These distinctions are not lost. Instead, a deeper understanding is added on to them. Through visualization the meditator comes to recognize that, in a sense, our inner and outer worlds are both 'real', or both 'dream', for external events and people and internal visualization are of the same nature: they are both *śūnya* – empty of inherent existence. Advanced practitioners have even been able to bring about seemingly miraculous changes in the external world through the power of their understanding of Emptiness.

We may worry that by entering the world of these visualizations we shall 'lose touch with reality'. Yet we all too easily forget the true nature of our everyday experience. We treat the world of the senses as though it was real and permanent when it is not. We may fall in love with someone and expect them to give us security, forgetting that when conditions change we shall be separated from them, or their feelings towards us may change. Inasmuch as events and people are in constant flux and ultimately ungraspable, our everyday life is like a dream, but we tend to ignore this and treat it as solid and reliable. At least if you fall in love with a visualization you are reminded each day of its true nature, as it appears and then disappears within the blue sky of Emptiness. Thus the visualization practices are like dramatic lessons in the nature of life and how to live. In the meditation we learn to enjoy and appreciate everything that appears to our minds, yet we also know that there is no point in trying to grasp the rainbow visions of Buddhas and Bodhisattvas. In this way we train our emotions to enjoy and aesthetically appreciate the everyday world without becoming attached to it.

As our practice of visualization deepens, increasing amounts of our energy will become engaged with the Dharma. When we first take up the practice of meditation, if we are honest with ourselves we usually see that our emotional energies are most strongly stimulated by basic experiences, such as eating and sex. This is where our emotions are anchored. Through visualization, we increasingly draw them away from these preoccupations and invest them in the meditation, until our emotional centre of gravity is a Buddha or Bodhisattva. As the figure we are visualizing is subtle, this causes our emotions to become more refined.

Finally, after years of visualization practice, we may concentrate on allowing the figure to dissolve back into the blue sky. Now all our emotions are invested in śūnyatā. We have detached them from the world of the senses, and even from the archetypal realm of symbols, and allowed them to dwell on Reality itself. In the blue sky our emotional energies expand freely, having lost their propensity for getting fixated on or 'locked onto' particular experiences, which is the cause of all our sorrows. It is this state of happiness, understanding, and freedom to which the practice of Buddhist visualization can lead us.

Four

Taking Up the Practice
of Visualization

We have seen that visualization of different Buddha figures is a potent method of self-transformation that can help us to make speedy progress on the path to Enlightenment. In the West these days it is easy to find books that give the texts and detailed descriptions of Buddhist visualizations. However, it is not enough to go to a library, find a sādhana, and start experimenting with it. To use these methods effectively we need to practise them within a very definite framework. In this chapter we shall examine all the elements that need to come together to make the visualization of Buddhist figures potent and meaningful.

Going for Refuge and skilful action

All Buddhist visualizations begin with the recitation of verses in which one commits oneself to go for Refuge and practise skilful action. These form the essential context for all Buddhist meditation, so we need to explore their significance.

The Buddhist path begins from an experience of unsatisfactoriness. We become aware that though ordinary life has its enjoyments it can never give us complete fulfilment. Some of the time we experience mental or physical pain and, even when we are happy and comfortable, because everything is impermanent we know (though it is all too easy to forget) that these satisfying states will change. Indeed, it is obvious (though again it is usually more convenient to forget) that life is a journey that ends in old age, sickness, and death. Most people are dimly conscious of these facts but, seeing no way of avoiding them, they bury their heads in the sands of pleasure and distraction. Thus, as Thoreau puts it, 'the mass of men lead lives of quiet desperation.'

In Buddhism, this world of unsatisfactoriness and actual or potential suffering that we inhabit is called *saṃsāra*. It is the world of repetitive patterns, of energy locked into habits. It is the world of impermanence, in which everything eventually turns to dust in our hands, and then finally our hands turn to dust. It is the world of duality, in which we as egos 'in here' confront a world of people and objects 'out there' from behind the barricades of our own loneliness and separation. It is called the 'endless round' because, according to traditional Buddhism, one can circle endlessly from life to life, entering wailing into life then, after an uncertain span, being carried out of it feet first, only for the momentum of our energies to precipitate us back into a new form of existence.

The repetitiveness and unsatisfactoriness of saṃsāra is vividly depicted in Buddhist art. In a symbolic painting generally known in the West as the 'Wheel of Life' (Sanskrit *bhavacakra*) it is portrayed as a wheel that turns forever. Its motive power is provided by three animals at its hub, moving ceaselessly as though on a treadmill. There is the cock of craving, the snake of hatred or aversion, and the pig of ignorance. They run on endlessly, each biting the tail of the one in front, in a kind of awful dance. Their interaction causes living beings to be reborn in one or another of six realms, which are depicted within the wheel. These are the worlds of heavenly beings, jealous titans, humans, animals, hungry ghosts, and hell beings. These can be interpreted literally, as six different realms into which one may be reborn, or psychologically, as different mental states – all of which are experienced by human beings. However you interpret them, none is permanent and none is completely satisfactory. They are all just aspects of the same dreary cycle.

This analysis of our existential situation might appear pessimistic, were it not that Buddhism categorically insists that we can break this circle and bring the wheel to a halt. We can awaken from the nightmare of the cock, snake, and pig. Craving, aversion, and ignorance can be replaced by tranquillity, love, and wisdom. We need not be subject to the tyranny of birth and death, need not be sentenced to spend a life term in any of the six realms. In fact, we can go beyond all restrictions whatsoever – even those of time and space. It is possible to be totally free. This achievement is permanent though not static – in a sense we might still be developing, but in a way inconceivable to human experience. The Buddha testifies from his own experience that there is a state of Enlightenment, attainable by any man or woman prepared to make the effort, that is permanently satisfying, and which banishes even the fears of old age, sickness, and death for ever.

This is a claim which we are not asked to take on blind faith. Buddhism encourages us to examine its teachings on the basis of our reason, experience, and intuition. Through looking at the lives and teachings of the Buddha and his Enlightened disciples we can decide for ourselves whether they are reliable witnesses to a state of Enlightenment. Do their lives exhibit the happiness and freedom that ours lack? Do their teachings square with our experience of life? We might try out Buddhist meditational methods and follow the Buddha's ethical precepts for a while to verify for ourselves whether they lead to more expansive and satisfying states of mind. Lastly we can consult our depths, our inner voices. Sometimes our intuition can leap to a certainty about something while our brains are still toiling to sift the evidence. We might find something deep within us responding to the Dharma, something which knows that life can have a deep meaning, that there is a seed of Enlightenment within us waiting to flower if we make the effort to tend and nourish it.

Out of this testing in the fires of reason, experience, and intuition we shall, I hope, forge a confidence that the Buddha is a reliable guide on the path to Enlightenment, and decide that we too will devote ourselves to following that path. At this point, to use the traditional terminology, we go for Refuge to the Three Jewels.

Going for Refuge is essentially the act of committing oneself to gain Enlightenment just as the Buddha and many of his followers have done. The Three Jewels or Three Refuges – the Buddha, Dharma, and Sangha – are what we rely upon in our quest. The Buddha Jewel is both the human historical Buddha and the state of Enlightenment which he attained and which we too can reach. The Dharma is the teaching of the Enlightened: all those explanations and methods developed within the

Buddhist tradition through which we can gain Enlightenment. In its widest sense, the sangha is the company of all those who are making use of the Dharma to become Enlightened. More specifically in this context it is the fellowship of all those who, though they may not yet be fully Enlightened, have had at least a glimpse, a flash of insight, into the true nature of things, and have thereby become reliable guides on the path to nirvāṇa.

The Buddhist path, then, begins with Going for Refuge, and one formally becomes a Buddhist by ceremonially reciting the formula of Going for Refuge in the presence of an ordained Buddhist. Essentially, though, Going for Refuge is not a matter of ceremony, nor is it just the starting point of the Buddhist life. In a sense, it is the whole of it. It is the conscious expression of a deep urge to grow beyond what one now is; a commitment to the continuing unfoldment of the creative potential within us. Hence it is not just the beginning of the path, it is the motive power, the engine that carries us along the path, which *is* the path. At every step of the spiritual path we go for Refuge more deeply, commit more energy to the quest for Enlightenment. Finally, with the attainment of Buddhahood, we shall become our own refuge, able to rely totally on the transcendental reality that shines through all our experience.

Sadly, the centrality of Going for Refuge has been somewhat lost sight of in some Buddhist traditions. This has had a number of unfortunate consequences. For example, Going for Refuge should be the criterion for deciding whether someone is effectively a Buddhist. When this is forgotten, the definition of a Buddhist is often drawn too widely or too narrowly. In some places, people may think they are Buddhists just because they have been born into a Buddhist family. Although this may give them a Buddhist cultural background, they may not be following the Buddha in any meaningful way – for the only meaningful way to be a Buddhist is to make some effort in the direction of Buddhahood. Others may identify being a 'real Buddhist' with a particular lifestyle, particularly that of the saffron-robed, shaven-headed monk. However, there may be many genuine Buddhist practitioners who for one reason or another are not following a monastic lifestyle. Nor, sadly, can we assume that all wearers of the saffron robe are making real efforts to develop wisdom and compassion. So the true test of whether one is a Buddhist is not one's lifestyle but whether one is making an effort to follow the Buddhist path of development.

This is not to say that lifestyle does not matter. The Buddhist path can be subdivided into the three stages of skilful action, meditation, and wisdom. A commitment to gain Enlightenment will find expression in ethical action. Buddhist ethics are based on motivation: actions initiated from states of mind rooted in peaceful, loving, and wise mental states are termed 'skilful', for they have beneficial consequences for ourselves and others and lead us closer to Enlightenment. Actions based in craving, aversion, and ignorance are 'unskilful'. They benefit no one and enmesh us more tightly in the web of saṃsāra. Skilful states of mind will naturally want to find expression in a lifestyle that is increasingly compassionate and aware.

Going for Refuge and Buddhist ethics provide the essential context within which all our interaction with Buddhist figures through visualization and devotional practices must take place. The figures themselves are all images of a Going for Refuge that has found its fulfilment. They all represent skilful states of mind raised to the highest possible power. One can only successfully interact with them on the basis of a genuine commitment to gain Enlightenment and practise skilful action. To do so for any other purpose would be useless; however clear one's 'visualization' might be, one would not really be seeing them at all.

I am stressing this because, sometimes, Going for Refuge, while not being dispensed with altogether, can be seen as the kindergarten of the Buddhist life, to be hastily left behind as one rushes to join the grown-ups and start receiving initiation into Buddhist visualizations. Going for Refuge is then reduced to 'square one' of the spiritual life, from which one can begin whizzing up the golden ladders provided by the 'short path' of the Buddhist Tantra and arrive at the dizzy heights of nirvāṇa in record time. But in spiritual development, even more than in the other aspects of life, haste and speed are often mutually opposed. I have found from my own experience that 'square one' is actually a difficult place to get to. Arriving there means no longer grasping after meditations and initiations that are supposedly 'powerful' and 'advanced'. On the occasions when I have managed to settle down happily in 'square one' and begun to explore it, I have found that all the other squares are contained within it.

The need for a teacher

As we have seen, the sādhanas all assume that those practising them are doing so as an expression of their Going for Refuge, and with a grounding in Buddhist ethics. In addition, to practise visualization sādhanas you need to be in touch with a qualified teacher. He or she can guide you with your meditation, resolve your difficulties in understanding, and help you come to terms with the changes in yourself that the practice brings about.

While not so many years ago Westerners would almost certainly have had to travel to the East to find a spiritual teacher, there are now qualified people in virtually every country in western Europe, as well as North America and Australasia. The choice of a spiritual guide is an extremely important one. It is also a decision for which we in the West have no training or relevant experience, and our criteria for deciding are often wrong. As with Going for Refuge, we need to use our reason, experience, and intuition rather than blind faith. To start with, we need to examine our motivation for looking for a teacher. Are we expecting to enter an authentic relationship with someone who can help us with the difficult work of self-transformation? Or are we hoping to find someone incredibly spiritually advanced who can sweep us to Enlightenment through their miraculous power?

The second of these motivations can only cause trouble. In essence, it is based on passivity and a childish wish to be taken care of, and it is very likely to end in tears. It is rather akin to people looking for something for nothing in the financial world, whose desire to find ways of making money without working makes them gullible. Presented with a dubious 'get rich quick' scheme, they are likely to accept it at face value because they so much want it to be true.

Because it places emphasis on the teacher's 'powers' it is easy for this motivation to lead one to choose a teacher because they are very charismatic, or because they make impressive claims. Neither of these is any guarantee of spiritual development. A genuine Buddhist teacher will not make claims in order to win devotees. Even statements that someone is part of a lineage of incarnate lamas or has received many teachings and initiations should not be taken as a guarantee of their abilities. One should beware of anyone who demands respect or devotion because of their status within a Buddhist organizational hierarchy or who makes much of their 'Buddhist credentials'. Such demands are essentially manipulative.

Here one has to try to discriminate between the actions of the teacher and those of their perhaps over-enthusiastic junior followers. Someone may be a genuine teacher, uncaring about fame and reputation, but some of their disciples may not have outgrown such things. Sometimes one hears conversations between disciples of teachers that are not much better than children's playground arguments of the 'my dad's bigger than your dad' variety. Competitiveness – basking in the reflected glory of one's teacher's fame, rank, number of followers, or supposed 'spiritual power' – is unhelpful to true spiritual development, and while a certain amount of it is almost inevitable, one would expect it to be strongly discouraged by a true teacher.

According to the Buddhist tradition, genuine teachers will attract disciples through four qualities.[6] First they will have a welcoming, generous attitude to people. Secondly they will be kindly, and speak in a friendly way. Thirdly they will be happy to teach the Dharma, taking the opportunities that arise to help people change. Lastly, they will 'practise what they preach', being (or at least working hard to become) exemplars of mindfulness, calm, selfless love and compassion, and wisdom. Someone choosing a teacher should use their judgement to see how far that person displays these four qualities.

Initiation

According to Tantric tradition, before taking up the practice of a sādhana one must (usually) receive the appropriate initiation or permission to practise from a qualified teacher. The Tibetans consider that without initiation most practices will be ineffective. They see initiation, especially the 'great initiations' known as *wongchen* in Tibetan, as more than ways of introducing someone to a practice and validating its authenticity. They believe that through correctly receiving the initiation one can gain access to a stream of spiritual energy that has been transmitted through a 'lineage' of previous practitioners of the sādhana. Thus one can also speak of Tantric initiation as 'empowerment'.

Buddhist Tantra is divided into a number of different levels, and the 'great initiations' are the gateways to the highest level of practice, known in Sanskrit as *anuttarayoga*. To attempt practices of this level of Tantra without the appropriate empowerment is considered by Tibetans to be not just a waste of time, but positively dangerous.

Personally, with regard to the lower levels of Tantra, I have no doubt that someone who was genuinely Going for Refuge and who had some previous experience of visualization could, if necessary, take up a new sādhana without initiation, practise it sincerely, and be successful with it. As for the practices of the higher levels of Tantra, I am absolutely in accord with the tradition. Visualization is not something to be played with lightly. It is like electricity. Used by someone qualified it can light up a whole house. An amateur tinkering around with it may give themselves a nasty shock. More likely, though, they will fail to make the right connections and remain stuck in the dark.

Receiving initiations – things to be aware of

Leaving aside questions of whether one can ever dispense with the formal permission to practise certain sādhanas, what is completely indispensable in order to practise Buddhist visualization is that you should *be* a Buddhist. Initiations are essentially aids to deepening your Going for Refuge by strengthening your connection with some facet of Enlightenment.

Seeing Tantric initiations as situations in which we can further our Going for Refuge can help preserve us from a number of mistaken ideas about receiving them. Firstly, it helps guard against the risk of seeing initiation in mechanical terms. It is common for both Tibetans and Westerners to talk of initiations in terms of their level and power. One hears phrases such as 'Oh, this initiation comes from a very powerful lineage' or 'Lama so-and-so is giving a very advanced initiation'. It is important to understand that these statements may only be true in theory. A lineage of initiation may stem from a teacher of very great spiritual maturity. An empowerment may be intended for those who are spiritually advanced. However, there is in Buddhism no equivalent of the doctrine of *ex opere operato* found in Roman Catholicism. The Roman Catholic Church believes that the efficacy of its sacraments is not dependent upon the spiritual development of the priest. But for Buddhism the effectiveness of the empowerment depends *entirely* on the state of mind of the guru and the disciples attending the ceremony. To put it bluntly, the initiation is only as good as the Going for Refuge of the guru and the disciples.

Emphasizing Going for Refuge also helps to prevent us from thinking of initiation as conferring spiritual status. Attending an initiation ceremony in itself guarantees nothing. Sometimes people in the West are given quite 'advanced' Tantric initiations. Though these may plant seeds which may fructify at a later stage in their development, they are not thereby magically transported to a higher state of spiritual insight. Unfortunately some people may not understand this and may use the fact of having received a particular initiation to puff up their egos and feel superior to those who have not. Concentrating on the depth and sincerity of one's own Going for Refuge, and simply examining whether the initiation has helped to deepen it, counteracts any tendency to ego-aggrandisement and competitiveness.

Lastly, concentrating on Going for Refuge prevents us from looking at initiation too narrowly. It is all too easy to think of empowerments as happening only in a set ritual context. I can vouch from my own experience for the inspiring nature of ritual empowerments – they can be a deep shared meditation between guru and disciple. Nonetheless it would be better to be open to the possibility of initiation in other contexts. Real Buddhist teachers do not just 'give teachings', they *are* the teaching. They are living exemplars of awareness, compassion, and skilful action. Hence any meeting with them, if we are sufficiently aware and receptive, is an opportunity to deepen our Going for Refuge. In fact we could see empowerment in even wider terms, as in a way the Zen tradition does. If an empowerment is essentially a situation that catalyses a deeper level of spiritual insight, then there are stories of Zen devotees receiving empowerments from stones and the sound of a tolling bell. If you are sufficiently awake to the nature of yourself and your surroundings, then life is offering you empowerment and new initiations all the time.

It cannot be stressed too strongly that you should make quite clear before receiving any initiation what it is that you are taking on. Someone I know once went along to a Tantric initiation in London 'because it was there'. Some time later he discovered that in repeating the liturgy in Tibetan he had unwittingly taken certain vows. Though he was full of good intentions, he certainly had not intended to make such commitments, and was quite disturbed by what had happened.

The point I have just made applies most strongly to initiations into the higher levels of Tantra. These almost inevitably involve taking on a number of commitments: to keep the Tantric precepts (known as *samaya* in Sanskrit), to do the six session yoga (a short meditation practice, so called because it must be performed six times each day), along usually with further commitments associated with the particular initiation – such as to recite the mantra of the meditational deity a particular number of times each day. These are serious commitments, and require time, dedication, and consistency. To fail to keep them would be likely to have adverse consequences, and make it harder to practise the Dharma in the future.

I hope that in the West we shall arrive at a point where everyone taking up a visualization is well prepared beforehand. Until recently, Tibetan lamas coming to the West have been in a difficult position. They have seen their tradition threatened with extinction after the Chinese invasion of their country, and have wanted to pass things on to Westerners as soon as possible. Often they have been on tour, and have not been able to stay long with their students, so they have only been able to give them rudimentary instruction. Now that more lamas have settled in the West, and it is clear that the Buddhist tradition is taking root here, one hopes they will feel able to go more carefully again. Within the Friends of the Western Buddhist Order with which I am involved, we usually only give visualization practices of Buddhas and Bodhisattvas to people who are definitely committed to the Buddhist path, and have laid a foundation by practising ethics and śamatha meditation for several years. This 'slow but steady' approach may not be what some impatient Westerners want, but it does produce results.

Taking up a sādhana

Though practising any sādhana sincerely will have a positive effect, different types of sādhana appeal to different personalities. Although they are all gateways to the same experience of Enlightenment, in the early stages different sādhanas feel like gateways to completely distinct worlds. One may be deeply calming, another may stir up strong energies. Some figures are gentle and approachable; others are powerful and appear threatening. The best situation is for you and your teacher to choose a practice appropriate to you as an individual, pooling your knowledge of you as a person and the various practices available.

As time goes on, it is possible to add further sādhanas to your original one. However, there is usually one figure that is the central focus of your spiritual practice. This is often referred to as your *yidam*. This Tibetan word literally means oath, vow, or promise, and denotes a figure to whose meditation you are committed. It is sometimes restricted to figures of the highest level of Tantra, but in general it is a useful word to apply to the Buddha or Bodhisattva visualization that you regard as your main practice. Buddhist teachers often suggest that if you take up further practices you should regard the new figures as your yidam appearing under different forms.

Fidelity to one figure is important. It is not uncommon for someone, after an initial burst of enthusiasm, to find that a practice has gone rather dull. Human nature being what it is, it is easy to feel that the problem lies with the meditation. You may think, for example, 'Oh, this practice of Tārā (the female embodiment of compassion) isn't working for me. What I'd really like would be something sharper, to help me develop wisdom and clarity.' So you take up the visualization of Mañjuśrī, the Bodhisattva who wields the flaming sword of wisdom. This goes wonderfully for a while, it feels exciting and different. Then, as the shine wears off it, your experience of this new meditation reaches a plateau. Eventually, if you are honest with yourself, you have to admit that it is about as good as the Tārā practice was. While there may be times when a change of meditation will be helpful, there is always a danger of avoiding the steady work of familiarizing your mind with a particular sādhana, and instead going hunting for new and allegedly more 'powerful' initiations and sādhanas.

Here again it is important to bear in mind that our efforts in meditation depend on a context of Going for Refuge and ethics. A sādhana is in essence a dramatic representation of the process of Going for Refuge. If our meditation is not going well, rather than jumping to the conclusion that the method is at fault we should examine whether we have set up the conditions upon which successful meditation depends. Are we really in touch with our commitment to the Buddhist path? If our meditation is dull, it may be that we have lost our motivation and need to rekindle our Going for Refuge. Also, meditation is simply a concentrated flow of skilful mental states. We should be working to develop these all the time outside meditation. Has our practice of ethics gone slack, so that our daily life no longer supports our meditation?

In this book there is no space to look at techniques for working with visualization. Some people find it relatively easy to visualize; others find it very hard – I know a number of people who have difficulty actually seeing anything in their sādhanas. However, the ability to produce visual images is only one aspect of sādhana practice, and sometimes 'visualizations' in which one does not see anything can still be quite effective. We can make an emotional connection with the meditation, and feel the 'presence' of the Buddha or Bodhisattva, without being able to see very much at all.

Visualization is a complex procedure. It is an art form whose materials are imagination, thought, feeling, and intuition. It takes years of work on our minds to become truly proficient at it. However, if we have set up the right conditions for practice as described in this chapter, even rudimentary attempts can catalyse a process of inner transformation. Then, with time and sincere practice, the sādhanas will become increasingly satisfying. Eventually it will be possible to produce a true masterpiece: the sublime harmony of all aspects of one's being.

Amitābha mandala

Five

Entering the Mandala

We have seen how, through contemplating his life and achievement, it is possible to meet Śākyamuni on different levels. We can imagine his *nirmāṇakāya*, thinking of him as he lived and taught in India. We can experience him in a more visionary way, as the *sambhogakāya*, as we did when we looked at the visualization sādhana in Chapter Two. Finally, through following his teaching we can gain insight into Reality, and come to the *dharmakāya* – the Truth of things, which is what makes a Buddha a Buddha.

As Buddhism developed, in the Mahāyāna and Vajrayāna at least, increasing emphasis was placed on the archetypal Buddha, the *sambhoga-kāya*. Undoubtedly this was partly because this level of experience of the Buddha was the most beautiful and moving. Yes, it can certainly be very inspiring to contemplate the Buddha's *nirmāṇakāya*: to see him struggling, thin and emaciated by his quest for truth; to watch him walking through the Deer Park at Sarnath, gentler than the deer, more fiercely determined than the five ascetics whom he has come to teach. To watch him making his final tour, his ageing body moving slowly along the dusty roads, can be deeply moving. Yet there is a feeling of incongruence. So little of the ocean of his qualities can be contained in his increasingly battered body.

Furthermore, the *dharmakāya*, for most of us, is a little abstract. Spiritual qualities can only bring forth a heartfelt response in us when they are given some kind of concrete expression. Buddhahood may be all very fine, but we can only truly love a Buddha.

For these reasons, as Buddhism developed, it was the *sambhogakāya* around which devotion increasingly centred. The lights went down on the *nirmāṇakāya* and *dharmakāya*, and the radiant figure of the archetypal Buddha, 'blazing with signs and marks', took the centre of the stage. In the Mahāyāna sūtras it is not the historical but the archetypal Śākyamuni who sits on the Vulture's Peak – a site in northern India near the town of Rājagṛha where the Buddha often stayed – teaching the Dharma through both words and extraordinary happenings created out of the depths of his meditation.

There was another reason for this concentration on the archetypal realm: it was on this level that the possibilities of new growth and expansion were greatest. Though you can make the details of the Buddha's life more vivid for yourself, you will always be limited to the plains and hills of northern India, to the life of one person. Since the *dharmakāya* transcends time and space it is bound to seem abstract. The realms of the imagination, however, are vast. You could explore them for ever without exhausting their treasures.

Because of this capacity for development, as Buddhists over the centuries meditated on the archetypal Buddha, more and more forms appeared. They sprang up profusely, like wild flowers, in different shapes and colours. They evolved. New varieties were discovered. Eventually the Buddhist tradition was decorated with a riot of colour and beauty. All these forms were expressions of the life and vitality of the Dharma. Through the centuries the seeds sown by Śākyamuni found fertile soil in the meditations of his disciples.

The five Buddha families

To begin with, two new Buddhas appeared (and here we are speaking the language of myth, not describing a historical process). These expressed the two great aspects of Enlightenment – Wisdom and Compassion. As people dwelt on those qualities as embodied in Śākyamuni, so they took on a life of their own, and became two new 'archetypal' Buddhas. Their forms grew out of his central figure, to flank him. In time, two more Buddhas appeared, whom we might call the Buddha of Generosity, or of Beauty, and the Buddha of Action. These took up their posts at the other two cardinal points around the central Buddha. It is these five archetypal Buddhas whom we shall be meeting in the next five chapters.

Although we can talk of them as a set of five separate Buddhas, in a sense there is just one Buddha. The four who surround him just emphasize different aspects of the one experience of Enlightenment. They are that total experience seen from four different points of view. It is like refracting light through a prism to give red, orange, yellow, and so on. All the wavelengths that you perceive as those colours were present in the original white light. However, splitting the light into the spectrum tells you more about its nature and gives you a new appreciation of it.

The four surrounding Buddhas in their turn began to be encircled by other figures. Each Buddha became the head of a 'family' of figures, each of whom expressed a further aspect of his qualities. These other figures are the Bodhisattvas and Tantric deities whom we shall meet in the second and third books in this series.

This division into five families gives us a pattern, a scheme into which we can fit nearly all the archetypal figures we shall meet in this series. This is very helpful, just as it can help us to make sense of the riot of flowers by being able to see them as members of species and families. The universe of the Buddhist Tantra is very complex indeed. If we understand the basic patterning of the five Buddha families (or *kulas* as they are known in Sanskrit), then we shall have a map to help us voyage through the Tantric world. That world is none other than the world of our own minds. When we understand the map or scheme of the five Buddha families, we shall grasp the patterning of the deepest levels of our own psyche.

As we shall see more fully in the the third book in this series, Tantric Buddhism developed a complex system of correlations which associated mundane things with transcendental (Sanskrit *lokottara*) qualities. By doing this, the Tantra achieved two aims. First, it reminded its practitioners that attaining Enlightenment does not mean going off to some other world. Rather we just have to bring about a radical change in our approach to our present experience. Instead of seeing mundane things as hindrances to be avoided, we recognize that, seen aright, 'this very place is the lotus paradise, this very body the Buddha'.[7] Secondly, through correlating mundane and transcendental, the Tantra made it possible for anything mundane to serve as a reminder of Reality.

The scheme of the five Buddhas provides a basic patterning for much of the Buddhist Tantra, so a great number of these correlations are associated with it. Understanding and reflecting on these will give us a key to much of the symbolism of the Vajrayāna.

Trying to connect with the correlations – to see why certain aspects of experience should be associated with one Buddha rather than another, is a frustrating but ultimately rewarding exercise. It is frustrating because Tantra is an 'organic' system; the correlations rarely fit into a neat logical scheme. Just when you have four aspects of something neatly assigned to four of the Buddhas, the fifth will often be bafflingly inappropriate. It is ultimately rewarding because reflecting on the correlations can spark off your spiritual intuition. If you meditate on all these correlations, you widen your view of existence, and you begin to make connections between aspects of your experience you had never seen before.

At the end of this book is a table of correlations. I have included a good number of the traditional ones, though certainly not all. (For instance, I have not thought it appropriate to include the Tantric pledges associated with the five Buddhas.) In discussing each Buddha I refer to many of the correspondences and suggest why they are appropriate. Some that I have not had the space to deal with in the text have been included in the table for the sake of completeness. In these chapters I have followed the system of the *Bardo Thödol* – sometimes known in English as the *Tibetan Book of the Dead* – a text of the Nyingma school of Tibetan Buddhism. Other systems of Tantric practice may correlate things in different ways,[8] but it should be helpful for newcomers to the world of the Vajrayāna to learn one system of correspondences as a basis from which to understand others.

The universality of the mandala

The map of the realms of the five Buddhas is arranged in a mandala pattern. The word 'mandala' has many meanings.[9] In its widest sense it can just mean a circle or concentration of energy, but for our purposes perhaps the most helpful definition is the taking of any facet of reality and surrounding it with beauty.[10] A mandala is a harmonious arrangement around a central point, a symbol of the harmony and integration of the different levels and aspects of our being.

The mandala is a universal symbol. It was one of the great achievements of Carl Jung that he showed the common patterns underlying the myths, legends, dreams, and visions of people around the world. Finding the same symbols and themes appearing in both 'primitive' and 'civilized' cultures, he demonstrated that the patternings of the deeper levels of the minds of all men and women are similar.

One of these symbols is the mandala. Mandala designs are found in sacred circles in magical and religious traditions. For instance, there are fine examples in the sand paintings of the Navaho people. Mandalas form an important aspect of both Hindu and Buddhist art and meditative practice.

More surprisingly, Jung found these mandalas when working with his patients. He identified the four main functions of the human personality as thinking, feeling, sensation, and intuition. In each person, one of these four would be the most developed. The four functions fell into two pairs, which were opposites. Whichever function was most developed, its opposite would be largely unconscious. So for someone whose intuition was most developed, sensation (the ability to relate to the world through the senses and aesthetic appreciation) would generally be underdeveloped. Similarly, someone who tried to approach things through thought and understanding would tend to be in precarious contact with their feelings.

These undeveloped 'inferior functions' would often manifest in dreams, or be 'projected' onto other people. Jung's goal was to catalyse the process of what he called 'individuation' – to make conscious these different aspects of the psyche and bring them into harmony. Patients in whom this process was nearing completion frequently dreamed of mandalas. These were usually circular patterns within which four aspects were arranged around a central point. The people who produced them usually knew nothing about Buddhism or Navaho people, they just found the mandalas within their own minds. Drawing or painting mandalas gave them a feeling of wholeness. They could not say why, but there was something deeply satisfying about those particular patterns.[11]

Personal mandalas

It can be a very helpful practice to draw what we could loosely call a 'mandala of our life'. In this exercise, we sit down with a large piece of paper and reflect on our life as it is at present. We look at all the different elements in it: work, relationships, family, friends, hobbies and interests, spiritual aspirations, and so on. Then we try to decide, being as honest as we can, which is most important to us. Whatever that is, we write it down in the centre of the paper. Then we take all the different things we have thought of, and put them on the paper, writing or drawing symbols for them. We place each one in a position which reflects its significance for us. The more important things take a central position in the mandala, those that are more peripheral go nearer the edges. We try to arrange the different elements so as to bring out their relationships to each other.

This can be a very useful exercise in itself. Seeing all the different aspects of our life laid out before us can provide a new perspective on it. We shall often recognize relationships between different parts of our personal mandala that we had not seen before.

Drawing up this personal mandala is only a beginning, though. The next stage is to consider how satisfied we are with it. Do we want some things to move closer to the centre – to give them more time and importance in our life? Is the mandala balanced, or does it need rearranging, or to have balancing elements added? Is what we have put at the centre of our mandala really the best thing for us to centre our life around? After considering these questions (perhaps talking them over with a friend) we can then draw a new mandala, the mandala of the next stage of our life, a mandala that comes closer to our ideal.

For the mandala to be satisfying, what goes at the centre is crucial. But we may find that our mandala has no clear centre. At one time or another different interests and concerns drift, or leap, into the centre, only to be displaced by something else. It is the feeling of there being a vacuum at the centre of their lives, nothing definite or worthwhile at the centre of their mandala, that oppresses so many people today. It is only when there is one consistent centre to our mandala that our life will develop strength, momentum, and a satisfying direction.

However, that centre cannot be just anything. For our lives to be deeply satisfying, what we put at the centre of our mandala cannot be an egotistical concern. Some people, for instance, put fame, riches, or sex at the centre of their mandalas. This gives their lives a clear direction, a single-mindedness, but finally, because all conditioned things are impermanent, the centre of their mandala caves in, 'Things fall apart, the centre cannot hold.'[12] Or sometimes they achieve what they wanted, only to find dissatisfaction still gnawing at them. There is a deeper centre to their psyche that they have never acknowledged, never included in their mandala, and, having ignored it, they feel its absence.

Following a spiritual path means putting some aspect of Reality at the centre of one's personal mandala. For a Buddhist, it involves placing Enlightenment at the centre, represented by Śākyamuni, or one of the other figures we shall meet in this book. Each of the figures we shall be meeting embodies an approach to truth, a path to freedom. They each represent infinite expansion and creativity. Placing one of them at the centre of our mandala opens the way to continuous development, ever-increasing freedom. Each figure represents what we can become if we fulfil the deepest potential of our nature, whereas putting ourself as we are now at the centre is a recipe for stagnation. It may feel safe and comfortable, but ultimately it will be a dead weight at the heart of the mandala, blocking our growth.

Ideal mandalas

Useful as this personal mandala exercise is, the potential of mandalas as tools for self-transformation goes far beyond it. Even the improved version of the mandala of your life that you finish up with at the end of the exercise may still be very far from satisfactory. There may be unresolved conflicts within it. There may be whole areas of your potential that are uncharted territory, hardly represented at all on the map of your life at present. There may be other parts which in former days might have had 'Here be dragons' scrawled across them – aspects with which you have not yet come to terms. Buddhism uses ideal mandalas as objects of meditation, to enable one to go beyond all these limited, unsatisfactory ways of being and to unfold the full potential of one's consciousness.

To visualize an ideal mandala has a powerful effect on the mind. On a conscious level, it can make you more aware of undeveloped aspects of yourself. Just as Jung found his patients relying on one psychological function at the expense of others, so on the spiritual level you can tend to keep on 'putting your best foot forward' until it is so far in front of the other that you are in danger of falling over! In an ideal mandala, all spiritual qualities will be represented in a harmonious pattern.

More than this, visualizing a mandala has a great effect on your energies. Through repeated meditation, letting the pattern and details of the mandala sink into your consciousness, the deeper energies of your mind begin to take on the pattern, like iron filings arranging themselves around a magnet. Meditating on mandalas often has a feeling of satisfaction to it, and a deep effect, that is very hard to explain. It is a basic principle of Buddhism that whatever you set your heart and mind upon, that you become. So if you repeatedly meditate on an ideal mandala, your mind increasingly takes on that harmonious pattern.

There is much more that could be said about meditating on mandalas. It is a central practice in the Vajrayāna. In the Buddhist Tantras, many thousands of mandalas are described. Some centre on just one figure; others include hundreds. For the purposes of this book, it will be enough to look at some features that are common to many mandalas, and then examine the world of the five Buddhas in detail.

Basic features of the mandala

When you see pictures of Buddhist mandalas, you may have the impression that they are two-dimensional. However, what is shown in *thangkas* and pictures is just a diagram, a ground-plan. Mandalas are really three-dimensional. They represent the residence of the Buddha or other figure whose mandala it is. It is rather like seeing a map of a stately home, together with its grounds and perimeter wall. However, the mandala is not open to spiritual tourists; to enter the 'divine mansion' at its centre you have to be planning to make it your home. In fact you have to aspire to become one with the Enlightened consciousness of the figure at the centre of the mandala. So let us explore the mandala a little, starting from the outside and working inwards.

The perimeter wall of a mandala actually consists of a number of concentric circles. The outermost is usually a great ring of flames. This forms a barrier that prevents anything from passing through. Well no, that is not quite true; you can pass through, but not without being transformed. In many religious traditions, flames represent transformation from a grosser to a subtler mode of being. In some religious traditions burnt offerings are made to the gods. Through this, it is believed, the subtle essence of what is being offered will be wafted upwards to the higher realm inhabited by the deities.

In general, fire is one of the clearest experiences of impermanence, the possibility of radical transformation, that we can have. I am writing this in the mountains of Spain, during the summer, when fire is a constant hazard. I am quite aware that, through someone's carelessness, the green pines and holly oak at which I am looking could be transformed in a few minutes into blackened stumps. Fire changes the nature of things, so for Buddhism it is a symbol of wisdom. Buddhism talks especially of the 'flames of śūnyatā' – the wisdom of Emptiness – for fire reveals to us that there is no inner essence to things that remains the same, behind the process of change. If you take ice and warm it, it will all become water; if you carry on heating the water, it will become steam. Fire demonstrates that there is just a process of transformation – water arising in dependence upon heating ice, steam arising in dependence upon heating water.

So the ring of flames symbolizes the transforming power of wisdom. It also shows us that entering the mandala involves being prepared to give ourselves up to a process of total transformation, after which nothing will remain of our old selves. To show that these are wisdom-fires, they are usually represented in five colours – the colours associated with the Wisdoms of the five Buddhas whom we shall soon be meeting.

If we pass through the ring of flames, we come to another protective barrier: a great wall surmounted by a tent-like structure, all made of stylized diamond thunderbolts, or *vajras*. These are one of the most important of all Buddhist symbols. They have the nature of both diamond – which is

63

extremely hard – and the irresistible power of a thunderbolt. They thus represent a fusion of the most dense and unbreachable with energy in its most ungraspable form. The vajra has the dynamic effect of a thunderbolt on other things, but cannot itself be affected. In Buddhism it becomes a symbol for Reality itself. More generally, it is a symbol for energy that cannot be stopped. Hence it represents the unshakeable determination and commitment needed to arrive at the centre of the mandala.[13]

In many mandalas of Highest Tantra, within (or outside) the vajra-tent we find the 'grounds' of the divine mansion. However, these are not quite what one would expect. At each of the four cardinal points and the intermediate directions is a great cemetery. These eight cemeteries, or cremation grounds, in which lurk beasts of prey, are symbols of the dangers of saṃsāra and the need for renunciation of attachment to its uncertain pleasures. Every feature within them has some symbolic meaning. For example, each one has within it a lake, which is understood to be filled with the water of compassion.

In addition, the eight cemeteries are associated with the transformation of different aspects, or levels, of consciousness. According to the Yogācāra school of Mahāyāna Buddhism, one can analyse the mind into eight different types of consciousness.[14] (The Sanskrit name for these consciousnesses is *vijñāna*.) First, there are the consciousnesses associated with the five senses: sight, hearing, smell, taste, and touch. Next comes the consciousness which perceives normal mental events, such as ideas, memories, and fantasies. Then on a deeper level comes the *manas* – this is the level of consciousness that apprehends things in dualistic terms – that interprets the world in terms of I and mine, self versus other. It is this mistaken interpretation that the Yogācāra identifies as the root of all our troubles. Lastly, the eighth consciousness, the deepest level of the mind, is known as the *ālaya* – which literally means store or repository. This level is called by the German writer Lama Govinda the 'basic universal consciousness'.

Cemeteries are places of death avoided by most people, but sought out by yogins and yoginis, who go to cemeteries and cremation grounds to confront fear, and to challenge death to appear. In facing up to the existential facts of life – which are also the facts of death – they bring about a radical revolution in their view of the world. Through contemplating impermanence they realize that seeing everything in terms of 'I' and 'mine', 'self' and 'other', is false. With this they undergo a 'spiritual death' – abandoning the egotistical interpretations of the *manas*. Thereby they accomplish what the Yogācāra calls a 'turning about in the deepest seat of consciousness'. Thus the cemeteries represent the next stage in the initiatory process of entering the mandala – the transformation of the eight consciousnesses through confronting death and giving up the view of separate selfhood. This limited view of oneself has to be 'dead and buried' – or here cremated – for one to experience the limitless consciousness of a Buddha and be ready to take one's seat at the centre of the mandala.

Before doing so, however, in some mandalas there is one more protective circle to pass through. This gentlest circle is a ring of lotuses. These symbolize purity and renunciation. The lotus renounces first the mud in which it was born and then the water in which it has grown, to open its petals to the sunlight – petals that are unstained by its earthy birth. So the lotus represents purity, and rebirth on a higher level. In all Buddhist art and practice the lotus is a symbol of the transcendental – of what has gone beyond the mud of the world, risen above even the gentle waters of mundane positive mental states, and now basks in the sunlight of Reality.

Within the ring of lotuses stands the divine mansion itself. This is usually four-sided, with a gate at each of the cardinal points. It is very beautiful, adorned with exquisite hangings and precious jewels. Its colour is often variegated to fit in with the symbolism of the mandala as a whole.

It is usual to enter a mandala from the east – which is the direction in which the sun rises to light the world anew. For this reason, in pictures of mandalas, the bottom is always the eastern direction (and not the south, as on most maps).

Mandalas, like houses, vary in their complexity. They may have just one level, or as many as five. Entering the divine mansion we may find many occupants or just one. Every aspect of the mandala – the protective circles, the residence and its inhabitants, its beauties and sometimes its seeming terrors – is understood to be an expression of the wisdom and spiritual qualities of the central figure. It is as though the main figure of the mandala is like a fountain, pouring outwards, its waters taking on different forms.

The realms of the Five Buddhas

As mentioned earlier, in the next five chapters we shall be entering the mandala of the five Buddhas. I am not going to describe their mandala as it appears in traditional visualization practices. Rather, I am going to treat it in a way that I hope will give more feeling for the different Buddhas, and the net of symbolism which connects them.

I shall not alter any of the traditional symbolism, or the relationships between the Buddhas, I shall just ask you to imagine that they are dwelling not in a palace, but in a world divided into five great realms. The five Buddhas are also known as the five *jinas* (conquerors), because they have overcome ignorance and entered the realm of Reality.[15] They are like five spiritual kings, each with his own territory over which he holds sway, teaching the Dharma.

We shall begin each chapter by journeying into the realm of one of the Buddhas, exploring it, and trying to gain a feeling for it. The symbolism associated with each Buddha is very distinctive, so that each territory is unique. In particular, each Buddha has a special Wisdom, an Enlightened view of existence. This Wisdom is the most important thing about him, so as we enter each realm we need to be looking for clues to the nature of the vision that he is trying to communicate to us.

Entering a mandala is an initiatory experience. Through it we can establish a new relationship with the depths of our consciousness, and understand more fully the nature of the world. This is not always easily come by. It often involves undergoing an 'ordeal' – a test of the seriousness of our intentions. Entering the mandala may not always be easy, but the spiritual treasures to be discovered in these realms will infinitely repay our efforts.

It is time we set sail for the eastern realm....

Akṣobhya

Six

Touching the Earth
in the Eastern Realm

You cannot remember how long you have been travelling. For so long now there has been just you, your raft, and the sea. It is night, and you are navigating by the stars. At times, gazing out into the universe, you feel as though the Earth is your raft, steering its course through the firmament towards some long-sought haven.

As night wears on, the seas become less boisterous, the winds more favourable, and you can sleep. In your dreams you are a prince or princess in search of your kingdom, there are spotlights shining on an empty stage. For a moment you are the spotlight, dazzling and brilliant. You are the stage, infinite in possibility. Then a white-robed figure steps onto the stage, into the brightness. He slowly opens his cloak at the chest. There is a universe inside his heart.

When you awake, the dawn light is brightening the sky and you can see land to the east. You steer towards it across a smooth, calm sea until eventually your raft noses forward into a gentle bay. The still waters in front of you reflect the outline of an extraordinary building. It is a palace, made of crystal, with lofty windows and high towers, filigreed with sapphire. It is strongly built, and battlemented with golden vajras.

Raising your eyes from the water's reflection, you look at the palace itself. Its gates are two huge semicircles, which mate into a full moon. They too are crystal, which reflect the water, your little craft, and you.

Gazing into them, you see things as they are, in their naked, ungraspable simplicity. You see yourself in that moment, without judgements, without accepting or rejecting anything – you are just another reflection in the moon gates.

Having given you their message, the gates swing open. You are entering the kingdom of the Buddha Akṣobhya ('immutable' or 'imperturbable'). You are being admitted to his Pure Land where everything is a reminder of the Dharma and an encouragement on the path to Enlightenment.

Akṣobhya is seated at the heart of his realm, on a vast blue lotus throne, supported by four massive elephants. The Buddha's body is made of deep blue light, the colour of the night sky in the tropics. He has dark hair, is dressed in flowing, richly ornamented robes, and sits in the full-lotus posture. His whole body radiates light. His left hand rests in his lap, totally relaxed. Standing upright on its palm is a golden vajra.

His right hand reaches down, palm inwards. The tips of the deep-blue fingers just touch the white moon mat on which he sits. There is something about the gesture which speaks to you. It is coming home, it is hitting the bedrock of existence, it is the answer to all questions. His whole figure conveys unshakeable confidence. He is so rooted that nothing could ever ruffle his composure.

He smiles, and the whole land understands. The special quality he transmits is wisdom. In understanding the meaning of that gesture, all the inhabitants of his Pure Land become wise, and enter a stage of the path to Enlightenment from which there is no falling back.

In his heart is a syllable made of pale blue light. It is the syllable *hūṃ* (pronounced 'hoong'), symbol of the integration of the individual and the universal. From his heart echoes the mantra which embodies his Wisdom. Its sound carries everywhere in his realm, slow and measured, like the call of a great drum: *oṃ … vajra … akṣobhya … hūṃ*.

The sound of the *hūṃ* has all the unshakeable certainty with which an elephant places its foot upon the earth. It has the same unalterable quality as the Buddha's fingers touching the ground. It is a stamp, a seal of

Reality, just as an action in a moment of time, once the moment is past, can never be erased or undone.

Seeing and hearing all this, your mind becomes absolutely tranquil and steady. Each moment is a total experience, which you feel in its full weight and depth. It lacks nothing; it is complete as it is. Everything is just a perfect reflection in the mirror of your mind.

Akṣobhya and the vajra sceptre

Now that we have entered the mandala, and come face to face with Akṣobhya (Tibetan *Mikyopa*), it is time we learned a little more about him. Devotion to Akṣobhya appeared early in Buddhist history and he plays a central part in several Mahāyāna sūtras.

In the *Akṣobhya Vyūha Sūtra*, Śākyamuni Buddha describes Akṣobhya's history. Ages ago, in a land called Abhirati (intense delight) a Buddha called Viśālākṣa was faced with a monk who wanted to vow to gain Enlightenment for the sake of all living beings. The Buddha warned him that he would be undertaking a daunting task, as to attain his goal he would have to forswear all feelings of anger. In response, the monk took a series of great vows: never to give way to anger or bear malice, never to engage in the slightest immoral action, and many others. Over aeons he was unshakeable (*akṣobhya* in Sanskrit) in holding to his vow, and as a result he became a Buddha of that name, and created a Pure Land or Buddha Field (Sanskrit *Buddhakṣetra*).

A Pure Land is a world that is the expression of the Enlightened consciousness of a Buddha. It is brought about through the infinitude of meritorious actions he has performed. It is a world in which exist the optimum conditions for making rapid progress along the path to Enlightenment. Many Mahāyāna followers centre their aspiration on being reborn in one or another of the great Pure Lands described in the Mahāyāna sūtras. Akṣobhya's Pure Land is represented situated an unthinkable distance to the east of our world, and like the world in which he first vowed to gain Buddhahood it is called Abhirati.

The description I have given of Akṣobhya's realm in the introduction to this chapter is designed to highlight qualities with which he is associated, rather than to follow the traditional description of his Pure Land. In the *Akṣobhya Vyūha Sūtra* Abhirati is described as a land in which palm trees and jasmine, stirred by the breeze, give off heavenly sounds surpassing all worldly music. It is a world in which everyone lives with joy in the Dharma, food and drink are abundant, and there is no illness. Its women are beautiful and 'never suffer the pains of menstruation'. Most important of all, whoever is reborn there attains the state of non-regression – they reach a stage of spiritual development from which Buddhahood is assured.

Perhaps the best-known sūtra in which Akṣobhya appears is the *Perfection of Wisdom in 8,000 Lines*. He is a particularly important figure in the Tantras because, like all Buddhas of the mandala, he does not stand alone, he is head of a *kula* or 'family' of spiritual figures. In his family are many of the 'high patron deities' (or *yidams* as they are called in Tibetan) of Highest Tantra.

Akṣobhya's spiritual family is called the Vajra family. The *vajra* (Sanskrit, *dorje* in Tibetan) is the symbolic diamond thunderbolt. In the previous chapter we found a wall of vajras encircling the mandala. Akṣobhya has a single vajra, as a diamond sceptre, standing upright in his left palm. It is an emblem of sovereignty, which is held by Indra, the king of the gods in Indian tradition. However, it is far more than just a sign of kingship.

The schoolboy riddle 'what happens when an irresistible force meets an immovable object?' has been answered by Tantric Buddhism. It just fused the two together to make the vajra. The vajra has all the immutable qualities of a diamond – so hard that nothing can make an impression on it. At the same time it is an irresistible force. It is an Eastern relative of the thunderbolt wielded by Zeus and Athena in the Greek myths, and of the hammer of Thor, the storm god of Norse mythology. It is the thunderbolt that can smash anything that crosses its path.

For Buddhism, it is transcendental reality that has these irresistible, immutable qualities. Everything mundane is mutable and changing, so the vajra becomes a symbol for Reality and, by extension, for the intuitive wisdom that realizes it. The vajra lends itself to the name for Tantric Buddhism – the Vajrayāna. This is the kind of Buddhism that takes the viewpoint of ultimate Reality as its starting point. In nearly all Tantric rituals the lama holds a vajra in his right hand. Many of the offerings in Tantric ritual are prefixed by the word 'vajra'. So one offers 'vajra-flowers' and so on. All this is a reminder to see everything in terms of its empty nature.

The stylized vajra used in Tantric ritual has four main parts. At its centre is an egg shape, representing the primordial unity of all things before they 'fall' into dualism. Emerging from each side of the egg shape are lotus flowers. With them is born the world of opposites, including the opposition between saṃsāra and nirvāṇa, ignorance and Enlightenment. From each of the lotuses protrudes the head of a strange animal, a *makara*. This is a kind of crocodile, whose amphibious nature hints at a meeting of conscious heights and unconscious depths. Then each end of the vajra branches out into a number of prongs. Usually there are four at each end, which finally reunite at the vajra's tip. Running vertically through the whole vajra is another prong. So if one looks at the end of a vajra what one sees is a mandala arrangement, usually with four spokes around a central point.

It is understood that one end of the vajra symbolizes the negative qualities that chain us to saṃsāra, the other for the spiritual qualities that free us. The great achievement of the Tantra is that its perspective is broad enough to unite the two. So the same axis runs through both mandalas. For the Tantra, even negative forces such as hatred and envy are seen simply as the pure play of Reality. Furthermore, it suggests that there are correlations between negative qualities and Enlightened Ones. Redirected, the energies tied up in greed, pride, and other unskilful states can be used to fuel our pursuit of Enlightenment.

To make this point as forcefully as possible, the Tantra associated every aspect of the mundane with a spiritual quality. For instance, looking at the table of correlations at the end of this book you will see that Akṣobhya is associated not just with wisdom, but also with the dawn, water, and form, and even with hatred, rites of destruction, and the hells.

The Tantra would never sanction hatred directed towards any living being. However, hatred can be redirected and used to further our development. When we are experiencing it there is often a kind of clear, cold precision to the way in which we see the faults of things. It is a state completely devoid of sentimentality or vagueness. We just have to see what the real enemy is. Once we hate suffering and ignorance, and are hell-bent on destroying them, that energy leads us to Akṣobhya's Pure Land rather than into the hells of violence and despair.

To examine all the different correlations with each of the five Buddhas would make this book very long indeed. I have hinted at some of them in describing their realms, others you can see and reflect upon in the table of correspondences. It is enough that we see the idea: that for the Tantra everything is a reminder, even an expression, of Reality. Dawn, blueness, even a glass of water, can all bring to mind Akṣobhya. When you see everything in this way, the ordinary world of appearances starts to become a Pure Land.

Touching the earth

Now that we have learned a little about Akṣobhya and the vajra, it is time to answer a question: How did Akṣobhya appear? How did a tradition of meditating on him come about? All these figures of archetypal Buddhas and Bodhisattvas are contacted in deep meditation. In withdrawing from the world of the senses, deeper aspects of the mind are given the opportunity to come into consciousness. The whole mandala is an expression of Enlightenment through symbols.

More specifically, the Akṣobhya tradition has two possible sources within the meditative experience. These are meditation on the historical Buddha and meditation on Emptiness. We shall look at each of these in turn. Both will lead us deeply into the world of Buddhist thought.

How did the Buddha Akṣobhya arise from meditation on the historical Buddha? As we shall see, each of the five Buddhas of the mandala embodies qualities possessed by Śākyamuni. This is as you would expect. As the essence of Enlightenment is the same in all times and places, all Buddhas will possess the same spiritual qualities, though they may express them in different ways. In the case of Akṣobhya, there is a strong connection between one of his qualities and a particular incident in Śākyamuni's life, known as the 'calling the Earth Goddess to witness'.

This is not a literal historical incident; it appears in Buddhist legend. That does not mean it is 'untrue', but just that it is attempting to convey another, more inward level of truth. This incident happened at the time when the Buddha was on the verge of attaining Enlightenment. Within the mind of the Buddha-to-be a drama of cosmic proportions was being played out. It is this psychic drama that the legend attempts to convey.

The legend describes Siddhārtha seated under his tree, striving to gain Enlightenment through profound meditation. The tremendous force of his effort soon drew the attention of Māra. In Buddhism, Māra is the personification of everything mundane, everything either inside or outside ourselves which binds us to the wheel of conditioned existence. His name literally means 'death'. The last thing Māra wanted was anyone escaping from his realm by gaining Enlightenment, so he launched an all-out attack on the meditating figure. He sent powerful armies against the Buddha. They deluged him with boulders and weapons. Yet he continued tranquilly meditating, and all the rocks, spears, and arrows, as soon as they touched the aura of peaceful concentration around him, just turned to flowers which rained down at his feet. Having failed to shift him by force, Māra sent his daughters to try to seduce him. But the Buddha did not even look at them. He just continued his inward search for freedom.

After these crude assaults had failed, Māra tried something trickier. He approached the Buddha and said, 'You are sitting on the seat on which all the Buddhas of old gained Enlightenment. By what right do you sit on that seat?' Tradition has it that all Buddhas gain Enlightenment on the same spot, the *vajrāsana* (diamond seat), which is the first point to solidify out of the swirling gases at the beginning of universal evolution, and will be the last point to dissolve away at its end. In terms of our current discussion, it is as though Māra said, 'You have seated yourself at the very centre of the mandala. Who are you to dare to sit there?' The *vajrāsana* is, perhaps, a little akin to the Siege Perilous of Arthurian legend – only someone of absolute purity can claim it as their own without mishap.

The Buddha replied, 'I have practised generosity, ethical discipline, and other spiritual practices for aeons, so I have earned the right to take my place here.' But Māra pretended not to be satisfied. He said to the

Buddha, 'You may say that, but who is your witness?' If the efforts of Māra's armies and his daughters represent the last waves of hatred and craving playing themselves out in the Buddha's mind, then this incident suggests a last subtle self-doubt. Perhaps the Buddha himself could hardly believe what he was on the point of achieving. Why him, of all men and women?

His answer to Māra was emphatic. He said nothing. Silently, with the fingertips of his right hand, he just touched the earth. In response, out of the ground in front of him sprang the goddess of the Earth. The Earth Goddess said, 'I will be his witness. I have seen him purifying himself for aeons through spiritual practices.' This was the Buddha's answer, and it finally put paid to Māra's efforts to deter him. He continued his meditation unhindered, and at last gained supreme and perfect Enlightenment.

It was perhaps through meditating on this incident in the legendary life of the historical Buddha that Buddhist yogins and yoginis made contact with the Buddha Akṣobhya. Dwelling on the qualities he exhibited, seeing them at their most potent, they came upon Akṣobhya. There is far more to it than the fact that Akṣobhya makes the same *mudrā*, the same gesture expressing a quality of Enlightenment, as Śākyamuni did when challenged by Māra. The interconnections and interplay of thought and symbolism within the mandala are very complex indeed. It is worth examining this incident and unravelling the threads further, to gain an idea of what is involved. By exploring this example, we shall gain more of a feeling for the multidimensional meaning of the mandala as a whole.

We have seen that the Tantra tried to subsume the whole of conditioned existence under one aspect or another of the mandala. Included in this are the different levels of consciousness possible for human beings. These different aspects, levels, or ways of functioning of consciousness are known as the *vijñānas*. *Jñāna* is a Sanskrit word meaning knowledge or wisdom. The prefix *vi* denotes separation. So a *vijñāna* is a consciousness – a way of knowing – that has fallen into duality, that experiences itself as a subject separate from an 'objective world' that it cognizes.

In the Yogācāra system of Buddhist thought, eight *vijñānas* are usually enumerated (as in the previous chapter, where we saw them associated with the eight cemeteries of the mandala). In the Tantra, each of these was then attributed to one of the five Buddhas. In this system, Akṣobhya is associated with the 'relative *ālaya vijñāna*'. This 'relative *ālaya*' has a very important function, which relates to a problem in Buddhist philosophy. Central to all aspects of Buddhism is the idea that actions have consequences. Skilful actions based on mental states such as love, wisdom, or tranquillity result in more fulfilling experiences. Unskilful actions based on craving, hatred, or ignorance lead to suffering. This is the Buddhist law of karma.

However, Buddhist thinkers were faced with a problem. How is it that a cause, such as a skilful volition based on generosity in the present, can bring about a pleasant effect in the future? What is it that links the two over time? Exploring the mind in meditation, the Yogācārins concluded that all our actions and mental states leave a trace at a very deep level of the mind. These traces are like seeds (Sanskrit *bīja*) which come to fruition one day when conditions are right. So none of our thoughts or actions is ever lost; they are preserved in the deep level of consciousness known as the 'relative *ālaya*'. The word *ālaya*, we have seen, means store; it can even denote a granary.[16]

We are now in a position to see a deeper connection between the incident of Śākyamuni's calling up the Earth Goddess and the Buddha Akṣobhya. When he answers Māra by touching the earth, Śākyamuni is pointing to the fact that he is ready to gain Enlightenment because the seeds of all the positive actions he has performed during aeons on the spiritual path are now going to come to fruition.

He calls as his witness the Earth Goddess, who rises up from the depths of his consciousness. The Earth faithfully preserves the marks of everything that happens upon it. Working down through its strata you can reconstruct its history. Every action has had its effect. The Earth is dumb witness to the lives and struggles of all human beings. It bears the scars of their building and destruction. It harbours their dust when the day is over. The Earth Goddess is a symbol of the *ālaya vijñāna*.

All this is made clearer if we read in the Pali canon the Buddha's own account of what happened to him as he sat under the bodhi tree.[17] First, he says, he entered meditative concentration. This corresponds to his over-coming the forces of Māra. In *dhyāna*, as meditative concentration is called, you move beyond the cruder forces of attraction and repulsion into a state of profound calm. After this, as we saw in Chapter One, flooding into his mind came memories of previous lives. He remembered endless births, with details of how he had lived and died in each one, and then taken new rebirth elsewhere. This psychological account is, surely, what the legend of the Buddha's calling the Earth Goddess to witness is expressing in the richer language of myth.

We can now see more clearly how closely connected is the symbolism of Akṣobhya with this aspect of the historical Buddha's Enlightenment experience. Having got this far, I even begin to wonder about Akṣobhya's symbolic animals. Is it really just a coincidence that the 'royal beasts' of the eastern realm are elephants, who, it is claimed, never forget? While that may just be a prank of nature, what is certain is that we still have one more step to take in unfolding the significance of the earth-touching mudrā.

Mirror-like wisdom

To do this we need to consider the symbolism of the elements in relation to Akṣobhya. With his rooted immutable quality, as he sits on his elephant throne, touching the earth, you might confidently assume that the element associated with Akṣobhya is earth. However, it is water. After you have been contemplating the mandala of the five Buddhas for a while, this will come as no surprise. As I suggested in the previous chapter, the mandala possesses an organic unity which goes deeper than the rational. Trying to fit together all the connections into a logical scheme is like trying to cram a large elephant into a somewhat smaller packing case. There is always some part which will not quite fit in.

Nonetheless, there is a rational explanation for Akṣobhya's association with water. This brings us on to the most important quality of the five Buddhas. Each of them embodies a particular Wisdom (Sanskrit *jñāna*) – an Enlightened way of seeing. This is their prime message. Meditating upon them, what we are really trying to do is come to a realization of the Wisdom which is their essential nature.

The special Wisdom to be found in the east, through meeting Akṣobhya, is the Mirror-Like Wisdom. With this Wisdom we see everything just as it is, impartially and unaffected. Hold up a red rose to a mirror, or a bloody dagger; it will reflect them both just as they are. It will make no judgements between the two reds, wanting to hold the first and flee from the second. Reality is just our experience, with no ideas added on. The mind perfectly reflects everything, but is not stained by it – just as the waters of a still bay can perfectly reflect a raft or a palace, without feeling any need to choose one above the other. It is this capacity of water to act as a mirror that makes it particularly appropriate to Akṣobhya.

We saw, in considering the vajra, that Akṣobhya encompasses the worlds of both saṃsāra and nirvāṇa – which, after all, are the same world seen with different degrees of clarity. So he is associated with the relative *ālaya vijñāna* in both its unpurified and its purified state. Before Enlightenment we grasp at 'external objects', reacting sometimes positively, sometimes negatively. All the time we thus put fresh seeds into the relative *ālaya vijñāna*. We create fresh karma to set the wheel of birth and death spinning into the future. Until we gain Enlightenment, the relative *ālaya* is the deepest level of the mind of which we can become directly conscious (and even that requires very concentrated meditation). However, when we pierce right through to Reality itself, we contact the absolute *ālaya*, the 'immaculate consciousness' (Sanskrit *amala vijñāna*), beyond space and time, beyond conditions, which knows no suffering.

Contact with Reality has a profound effect on the mind, and precipitates a total reorganization within it. Up to this point, subtly or grossly, we have been under the sway of our sense consciousness, caught up in the struggle to survive in the world. Now everything changes, and there occurs what in the Yogācāra is called the *parāvṛtti* – the 'turning about in the deepest seat of consciousness'. From now on, our psychic centre of gravity is the absolute *ālaya*. Contact with the absolute *ālaya* cures us of the delusion that we live in a world of duality, cut off from the outside world. With the *parāvṛtti* we perceive that everything is the product of the One Mind. (This is following the view of the Yogācāra school, which was also known as Cittamātra, or Mind Only.)

The realization that duality is a dream affects the relative *ālaya vijñāna*. It changes from being a *vi-jñāna* (operating within the subject–object delusion) and becomes just a *jñāna* – a non-dual wisdom. Specifically, it transforms into the Mirror-Like Wisdom of Akṣobhya. An Enlightened person continues to act, but he or she no longer creates karma. Karma comes about from the action of a subject on an object. Putting it crudely, you push the universe and sooner or later it pushes you back, but when concepts of 'you' and 'the world' have both disappeared there is just a perfect dance, with no separate entities to bump up against one another, no friction.

None of the reflections in a mirror stick to it, none are repelled by it. The mirror never reacts. It always stays imperturbable, immutable. Reaching this stage of practice, producing no new karma, serenely allowing the drama of birth and death to play itself out for the last time, you have entered the Pure Land of Akṣobhya.

Meditation on emptiness

Lastly, we need to look briefly at another possible means of encountering Akṣobhya. This is through meditation on śūnyatā. As we have seen, this term, central to both Mahāyāna and Vajrayāna Buddhism, means emptiness. The essential nature of everything is śūnyatā. When reading some older books on Mahāyāna Buddhism in which the term is poorly explained, some people gain the impression that this 'emptiness' or 'voidness' is a kind of nothingness. They get the idea that Buddhism is nihilistic, that śūnyatā is a kind of black hole at the centre of its philosophy, sucking the life and colour out of everything. Nothing could be further from the truth.

Śūnyatā is essentially the denial of the idea that we can ever capture our experience in words and concepts. We ponderously stick labels onto fleeting experience. I call myself 'Vessantara' through thick and thin, despite all the variations in my physical and emotional state, all the ups and downs of my consciousness. I get so used to being Vessantara that I come to assume that it stands for some fixed reality, which remains permanent behind the varying flood of my experience. Buddhism denies the existence of any fixed, unchanging entity standing 'behind' experience.

Everything is śūnyatā, devoid of any fixed nature. As we saw in Chapter Three, far from being negative, this aspect of Reality makes infinite development possible.

An understanding of śūnyatā puts everything in its proper perspective. We see that the things we fear and grasp after are all fleeting and insubstantial, like reflections in a mirror. We can then let them come and go, without worries. The transition to the world of śūnyatā comes about when we start believing our direct experience more than our concepts about the world. Our concepts are fixed and rigid. All too often we try to distort or deny our experience, to make it fit the Procrustean bed of our ideas about the world.[18] Through this we cramp ourselves, and cause ourselves endless frustration.

So when we meditate upon śūnyatā, we can arrive at the experience of Akṣobhya. Though each of the five Jinas is associated with an aspect of Wisdom, it is Akṣobhya who is particularly the embodiment of Wisdom in general. Thus to meditate on śūnyatā is to enter the crystal eastern gates of the mandala. There we see the deep-blue figure of the Immutable Buddha, holding the thunderbolt sceptre of Reality which smashes through all our ideas and concepts about it. At the same time, the dark-blue fingertips of his right hand touch the earth, the earth of direct experience, which is the only thing upon which any of us can finally rely.

Ratnasambhava

Seven

The Wish-Fulfilling Jewel
in the South

The sun is climbing overhead. It is time to travel on round the mandala, following the sun, to come into the southern realm. To arrive at the southern gate you will have to cross a great desert. You set out on foot with a servant, an aboriginal. At first there are trees and shrubs, then nothing: just sand. The desert winds pile it into extraordinary shapes. There are sand waves, sand fortresses, sand statues, sand rivers between banks of sand. The sun sparkles on it. Time passes, yet the sun seems to hang directly overhead. Sometimes, in the distance, herds of wild horses pass. It is getting very hot and very dry. You remember tales of people lost in the desert. You begin to feel as though you are made of sand. It is in your teeth, in your hair – the sand is taking you over.

Your servant offers suggestions. You don't listen – you have your map and compass, and perhaps you are too proud to take advice. You are prospecting for jewels. No, not jewels, just one jewel. You were told as you left the eastern realm that in the south you would find a wish-fulfilling jewel, a jewel which, like Aladdin's lamp, would grant all your desires. It is the gift of Ratnasambhava, the Buddha of the south – whose name means 'born from the jewel'. You trudge on. From time to time you see something that you think will satisfy your wishes embodied in a place or a person, but they all turn out to be mirages.

Finally there is nothing left. You are lost. The palace of Ratnasambhava is no nearer. Your servant is still moving along easily beside you, casting occasional anxious glances in your direction. He seems unhurried and unworried. You swallow your pride – the only thing you can still swallow – and ask him if he knows where you are, knows where to find the wish-fulfilling jewel. He looks surprised. Didn't you know? You had seemed so sure of yourself that he had assumed you did, but then why else would you give yourself such suffering? The wish-fulfilling jewel? Why he'll give it to you. He picks up a grain of sand and places it carefully in the palm of your hand.

Is this a joke? Could he have picked out one particular grain from all the others? No. It sits in your hand, glittering in the sun. You feel ridiculous asking a grain of sand to grant your heart's desire. Nonetheless, your servant is looking at you expectantly. You have nothing to lose. You make a wish to enter the southern realm of the mandala, known as 'the Glorious'.

Instantly you are standing in a vast and fertile plain. In all directions ripe wheat is waving in the gentle breeze. Your thirst has disappeared. Ahead of you is a palace. It is not huge and imposing, but beautifully proportioned and regular. It is built on a human scale, like the temples of ancient Greece. It is made of gold, and studded with jewels and semi-precious stones. You approach the gates. They are golden yellow, and stand four-square.

Inside there is great abundance. There are riches everywhere. Tropical vegetation casts flowers in myriad forms at your feet. Your path is made of jewels. Within the palace, all is abuzz with creative activity. Poets, musicians, artists, and sculptors are all producing works in praise of the figure who sits at the centre of it all. They follow his every movement like sunflowers constantly turning to face the sun.

The yellow Buddha Ratnasambhava sits on a great yellow lotus throne, supported by four horses. In his left hand, which rests in his lap, he holds a beautiful jewel. His right rests on his right knee, palm outwards, in a gesture of supreme giving. His generosity is limitless. He provides everything the dwellers in his Pure Land could wish for. He supplies the materials for all the artists and writers in his realm. It is the golden light emanating from his body that causes the profusion of growth in all the plants and foliage. Being in his world, you feel an abundance of energy and creativity, an overflowing happiness. You feel love and wisdom increasing, like plants growing in fertile soil.

Sameness and equality

Through imaginatively entering the realm of Ratnasambhava (Tibetan *Gyalwa Rinjung*), we should have gained an idea of the special Wisdom that he embodies. He transforms pride into the *samatā-jñāna*, the Wisdom of Sameness. After the sharp clarity of Akṣobhya's dawn, everything has blended into the haze of noon – the time of day associated with Ratnasambhava. His brilliant light softens the edges of the landscape's features; everything is honeyed by his golden radiance. His Wisdom brings out the common features of experience. It sees all aspects of life, all the myriad forms it takes, as marked with śūnyatā – all equally devoid of any inherent existence. It also sees the 'common humanity' in all men and women, and cares for them all equally. Thus Ratnasambhava is particularly associated with the human realm of the Wheel of Life.

As well as 'jewel born', Ratnasambhava's name could also be translated 'the jewel-producing one'. He is associated with riches, and is sometimes described as the Buddha of Giving. Being infinitely rich, he makes no distinctions of worth, giving freely to all. All beings are equally precious. After all, Ratnasambhava is associated with the earth element, and earth is the great leveller. Whatever our social position, whatever our race or sex, whatever our life-form, even, we are all made from the common clay. The golden sunlight of Ratnasambhava shines equally on palace and dung-heap. Through contacting his Wisdom we develop a solidarity with all forms of life.

Ratnasambhava's qualities bring to mind several images suggestive of pride being levelled, and the assertion of what all life has in common. There is Shelley's sonnet 'Ozymandias', in which he meets a traveller who tells him of coming upon the remains of a vast statue in the desert. The inscription on the pedestal reads:

> My name is Ozymandias, king of kings:
> Look on my works, ye Mighty, and despair!

The statue is a total ruin. As the traveller wryly observes:

> Nothing beside remains. Round the decay
> Of that colossal wreck, boundless and bare,
> The lone and level sands stretch far away.

I think, too, of the French aviator, Antoine de Saint-Exupéry. After crash-landing in the Sahara, he and his mechanic walked for days, desperate for water, and seeing mirages. Finally in the distance they both saw signs of a caravan. A Bedouin appeared in the distance. He was not looking in their direction, and they were both too far gone to call out. They knew that if the Arab turned his head forty-five degrees they would live; if not they would die. Slowly he did, and he saw them. He gave them water, and Saint-Exupéry describes his lifelong feelings for that nameless Arab, who was no one special, just another human being, a fellow journeyer through life.

Then there is the Midas myth. King Midas is a sad caricature of Ratnasambhava. He, too, is associated with both riches and equality. Everything he touches turns to gold. However, he destroys the humanity of things; even his family and his food turn to gold at his touch. His avarice estranges him from the human realm. His power of wealth becomes a torment for him.

The Wisdom of Sameness gives equanimity. We experience the 'eight worldly winds' – gain and loss, fame and disgrace, praise and blame, pleasure and pain – as equals, knowing that to chase one will be to lay ourselves open to the other. As we learn to treat each of these 'twin impostors' with calm impartiality, they lose their hold over us. We become like the earth, which receives all equally. We can do this only if we cease to relate to things personally, and see their advantages and disadvantages. To do this we need to find one more aspect of sameness: the equality of ourselves and others. The Wisdom of Sameness is not a cold meting out of equal justice. It is a strong positive identification with all life. Ratnasambhava's golden light dissolves the boundaries of self and other. When these disappear, all sense of property and ownership vanishes. Then you just share with others – without even any sense of giving, because giving requires a 'self' to give and 'others' to receive.

Riches and the wealth mentality

In Buddhist tradition, Ratnasambhava has not so far taken on a great deal of importance outside the mandala of the five Buddhas. While figures like Amitābha and Vairocana are known throughout northern Asia, and have devotees and sādhanas unconnected with their appearance in the mandala, Ratnasambhava's cult of devotion has yet to flourish. However, there are several reasons for thinking that with the establishment of Buddhism in the West his time has come. He possesses a constellation of qualities and associations that could appeal strongly to people in an industrialized society.

We have already mentioned his association with wealth and riches. His emblem is the jewel, and he is head of the Ratna (or Jewel) family. With his gesture of supreme giving (the *varada mudrā*), open palm turned outward, he showers the world with precious things. For people who have cut their teeth on consumerism and materialism, he offers a familiar and attractive gateway to the Dharma.

This symbolism of wealth and riches is emphasized by the figure of Jambhala (Tibetan *Dzambhala*), who is a member of Ratnasambhava's retinue in his Jewel family. In some areas of the Buddhist East, Jambhala came to be popularly regarded as a god of wealth. He is usually depicted as a large, even portly, figure who looks rather like a prosperous merchant. In his left hand he holds a mongoose, which he squeezes. As he does so, jewels pour from the creature's mouth. It is not unknown for people to meditate on Jambhala to help them out of financial troubles. Personally, I am prepared to believe that this magic *might* work.

However, you may be wondering what all this has to do with Buddhism. Jambhala is a Bodhisattva – a highly advanced spiritual being, Ratnasambhava is a fully Enlightened Buddha. There has to be more to their practice than getting rich on the Stock Market. So let us look at the different levels on which the symbolism of wealth can be understood.

On the most basic level, a Buddha or Bodhisattva wants to relieve people's suffering, even their everyday suffering. So if wealth will make them temporarily happy, then let them be given wealth. In his *Bodhi-caryāvatāra*, the great Buddhist poet Śāntideva says, 'For all creatures, I would be a lantern for those desiring a lantern, I would be a bed for those desiring a bed, a slave for those desiring a slave.'[19]

However, in meditating on Ratnasambhava one begins to obtain some of his spiritual riches – he is very generous with them. Dwelling on his shining yellow figure, with its jewel in one hand and mudrā of giving, one begins to feel a greater expansiveness in oneself. The essential change that Ratnasambhava brings about, on increasingly subtle levels as one's meditation deepens, is to effect the shift from a poverty mentality to a wealth mentality.

All too often we are concerned with a sense of lack in our lives. We do not have enough money, we are not attractive enough, we need a bigger house, and so on. Once we move onto a spiritual path, the blaring demands of our physical wants begin to subside. We are prepared to live a simpler life. However, we usually still feel a sense of lack, now transferred to the spiritual plane. This is what Chögyam Trungpa called 'spiritual materialism'. Still with our sense of lack, we go in search of more blissful meditations, a more famous guru, a more powerful teaching.

But we are still looking in the wrong place for satisfaction. We are still driven by an inner poverty to find some external riches to fill us. Meditating on Ratnasambhava changes this feeling. We see him pouring spiritual riches endlessly upon the universe, without a moment's thought for the possibility of running out of reserves. He is the endless benefactor, patron, philanthropist, host. Because his source of riches is unconditioned Enlightenment, he has access to an infinite reservoir of spiritual energy. So the thought of being careful, of hoarding what he has, rationing and allocating priorities, never occurs in his Pure Land, called 'the Glorious'. Everything in his realm flows in abundance. He is rich 'beyond the dreams of avarice'.

Through developing on the path of Ratnasambhava we soon feel no material lack. We realize that the higher world of the spiritual can give us the endless satisfaction that a Mercedes and a penthouse flat never could. Our own mind is a source of endless riches. As our development continues we mine deeper within ourselves, and from the ore of our direct experience we smelt more and more precious qualities.

Plate One Śākyamuni Buddha

Plate Two The Mandala of Vajrasattva with Śākyamuni and four of the
five Jinas above, and the three family protectors below

Plate Three Amitāyus

Plate Four Amitābha   *Plate Five* Vairocana
Plate Six Akṣobhya   *Plate Seven* Ratnasambhava

Plate Eight Amoghasiddhi with consort

Plate Nine Thousand-Armed Avalokiteśvara

Plate Ten Four-Armed Avalokiteśvara

Plate Eleven Mañjuśrī

Pride, humility, and the way into the human realm

The symbolism of the jewel (Sanskrit *ratna*, Tibetan *rinchen*) in Buddhism is extremely rich. It immediately calls to mind the Three Jewels, the three things which Buddhism holds most precious: the Buddha, the Dharma, and the Sangha. It is by committing yourself to centre your life around these three, in the ceremony of Going for Refuge, that you become a Buddhist, and formally set out on the path to Enlightenment. By Going for Refuge you set the Three Jewels at the centre of your personal mandala, until their radiant light has penetrated and transformed every part of it.

However, although faith in the Three Jewels is crucial to any progress along the spiritual path, there is a fourth jewel in which we need to have some faith. That jewel is ourselves. We have to believe that this unlikely lump of carbon that we are at present can be transformed into a spiritual diamond. Without at least a certain basic faith in our potential as human beings the whole thing will not work.

It can be quite easy to appreciate the wonderful qualities of those Three Jewels: the golden yellow Buddha jewel, the deep-blue Dharma jewel, and the ruby-red jewel of the Sangha. However, if deep down we see ourselves as untransformable, then our Going for Refuge becomes a game. We admire the Three Jewels from afar, and make token efforts to stick bits of tinsel onto ourselves to pretend we are becoming brighter. In reality, though, very little is happening.

As we saw earlier, the poison associated with Ratnasambhava is pride. However, pride is one side of a duality of which the other is always present. Where you have pride and a conscious over-valuation of yourself, hidden in the basement of your psyche is a great deal of insecurity. Similarly, within every Uriah Heep there is usually a well-concealed egotist to be found. Ratnasambhava's *samatā-jñāna*, his Wisdom of Sameness, shows us that whether we play high status or low the result is the same. We are still overly concerned with ourselves.

He also shows us the way out. He is supremely generous, and it is not possible truly to give without awareness of others. Giving takes you beyond yourself. It involves seeing the needs of others, and what will satisfy those needs. Through awareness of others we enter the human realm, which as we have seen is the realm of the Wheel of Life over which Ratnasambhava presides.

The human realm is the realm of cooperation. Here you come into relation with others, and no longer feel the isolation of pride. It is the only realm in which you can naturally feel the support of others, and hence escape both pride and lack of self-esteem. It is also the only realm in which you can empathize with others. Empathizing with them, you become rich in their riches. So it is the world of 'rejoicing in merits' – appreciating the good qualities of others and rejoicing in their happiness – of which Ratnasambhava seems to be the patron.

Culture and beauty

Another reason Ratnasambhava is likely to become a popular figure in Western Buddhism is that he is associated with aesthetic appreciation. Sangharakshita characterizes him as the Buddha of Beauty. This is a very important aspect of spiritual life. Sages and yogins from the time of the Buddha onwards have sung songs in appreciation of the natural beauties of the places where they lived and meditated. All Buddhist traditions have tried, each in their own way, to make their shrines, temples, and hermitages aesthetic and harmonious. Zen temples have their spare, spacious beauty, Thai temples their sweeping shapes and gilded pinnacles, Tibetan shrines their profusion of images and *thangkas*, sometimes overspilling like an avalanche of the archetypal into the everyday world.

This beauty and richness is more than an expression of devotion to the Three Jewels. The contemplation of beauty has a refining and transforming effect on our emotions, which are often tied up in quite basic needs and wants. It is not easy to make the emotional leap from enjoying these relatively coarse satisfactions to deriving our emotional sustenance from the archetypal realm of Buddhas and Bodhisattvas. We need gradually to wean ourselves off the one and learn to nourish ourselves with the other. This is where culture and the appreciation of beauty in nature and the arts has its place. Through dwelling on natural beauty, or on great artistic works such as those of Shakespeare, Bach, Michelangelo, or

Raphael, our energies become more refined. From being human animals, we climb towards the peak of human achievement from which it is relatively easy to take the fathomless leap into the sky of Enlightened consciousness.

In much of the East, Buddhism did not encounter developed cultures as it spread. Only in China did it meet with a society which had very refined forms of art and literature. Usually, Buddhism brought culture and learning, as well as teaching the path to Wisdom. The indigenous arts and culture, such as they were, were soon superseded or subsumed under Buddhist forms.

However, in coming to the West, Buddhism is encountering a culture that can trace its development through 2,000 years back to classical Greece. It is not really practical for most Westerners to ignore their cultural roots and simply take on an Eastern culture. A dialogue has to take place, and bridges will have to be built, between Buddhism and Western culture. This process will include identifying Western writers and artists whose work has some glimmer of the Dharma within it. On the other hand, Western culture is itself going to learn from Buddhism, and this could well produce a new flowering within it. After all, the discovery of the culture of ancient Greece brought about a renaissance in the West. How much greater could be the achievement of those Western artists, poets, sculptors, and dramatists who respond to the discovery of the Dharma! In all this, Ratnasambhava will sit pouring out fresh beauties and inspiration. He will give out spiritual jewels like an Enlightened Lorenzo de' Medici, presiding over a new rebirth of the human spirit.

Abundance of time and energy

Ratnasambhava also holds the antidote to a modern Western malady. As competition for jobs and trade becomes fiercer, people in the Western world find it harder just to stop, relax, and do nothing (without turning on the television). We are too 'full of care' to have the time to 'stand and stare'. Boxed in by skyscrapers, we miss out on cloud patterns and stars. Sitting in slow traffic, late for appointments, we hardly notice our surroundings. However, Ratnasambhava's whole attitude is one of superabundance, including that of time. He encourages us to take the time to experience the world around us, trying to see it through the eyes of his Wisdom of Equality. Then we may have something of the vision of William Blake:

> To see a World in a Grain of Sand,
> And a Heaven in a Wild Flower,
> Hold Infinity in the palm of your hand,
> And Eternity in an hour.

This surplus of time relates to Ratnasambhava's world being one of artistic creation. From the point of view of human survival, the arts are a luxury. We could exist without music, theatre, novels, or sculpture. They have tended to flower in times of wealth and leisure. (Incidentally, the same is true of spiritual life – India at the time of the Buddha was a wealthy society with a surplus that could feed thousands of wandering ascetics and holy men.)

Ratnasambhava shows us the way to open ourselves up to a wider world. The mandalas of our lives are often constricted, limited by our grim determination to get what we want. We spend most of our time aware of things and people only in terms of their use-value, especially their usefulness to us. Of course, we cannot neglect the practicalities of life; we need to get things done. However, if we are to be happy, our utilitarian concerns must be allocated a small and not too central place in our personal mandala. The greater part of our mandala should be reserved for an aesthetic appreciation of life, in which we value things for what they are in themselves.

The difference between these two attitudes is well exemplified by the reactions of two visitors to London early in the nineteenth century. The poet Wordsworth, standing on Westminster Bridge early one morning in the summer of 1802, wrote the famous sonnet beginning,

> Earth has not anything to show more fair;
> Dull would he be of soul who could pass by
> A sight so touching in its majesty:

A decade later the Prussian field marshal Blücher, surveying the same city, was moved to exclaim, 'What a place to plunder!'

Ratnasambhava, then, encourages us to develop a more aesthetic appreciation of life. A good way to work at this is regularly to set aside time to contemplate some kind of natural beauty. Part of the reason people relax in natural surroundings is that, as well as being peaceful and visually pleasing, they do not stimulate the tendency to utilitarianism. You cannot use or possess a sunset; you can only appreciate its beauty and allow it to enrich your spirit.

Taking this a little further, we could also associate Ratnasambhava with ecology and environmental concerns. He is connected with the earth, fertility, and the flourishing abundance of life. Also, it is he who holds the antidote to pride, and it is the hubris of the human race that is causing irreparable damage to our beautiful planet. His wisdom can teach us to appreciate the Earth aesthetically, rather than constantly looking for new ways to exploit it.

This superabundance of Ratnasambhava leads us to associate him with another quality, which has connections with aesthetic appreciation. That quality is playfulness. Play is a sign of spare energy, and of a wider perspective than is needed for the task in hand. It is creativity without any object in view beyond itself. As such, it can be a celebration of human consciousness. The energy that pours from Ratnasambhava, the ebullience of spiritual riches, gives us free energy and an expansive, relaxed vision. Out of this we can play – without needing any reason or justification.

Something of this abundance of energy is symbolized by Ratnasambhava's animal, the horse. The horse is an animal that can be tamed to become docile and obedient to the human. It puts all its raw energy under the direction of a human consciousness. On a deeper level, the horse is a symbol for the subtle energies within the human body that can be brought under control and refined through meditation. This symbolism is embodied in the figure of the windhorse (Tibetan *lung ta*). The windhorse is shown in Buddhist iconography as a kind of messenger, a little like Pegasus, the winged horse of Greek mythology. Though he has no wings, the windhorse flies through the air, carrying on his back the precious Three Jewels.

The wish-fulfilling jewel

To close this chapter, we need to look once more at the jewel that Ratnasambhava holds. Although it can be related to the appreciation of beauty, and pouring the wealth of the Three Jewels upon the world, there is a further level to its symbolism. The jewel the yellow Buddha holds is a wish-fulfilling jewel. In Indian mythology we find many objects which grant all desires – there is a wish-fulfilling tree, and even a wish-granting cow, but the most important one found in Buddhist icon-ography is the *cintāmaṇi* – the jewel that gives you all you could wish for. In Buddhism it became a symbol for the Bodhicitta – the compassion that impels us to gain Enlightenment for the sake of all living beings.

It is as though Buddhism says, 'You have been searching all through your life for fulfilment, in money, sex, companionship, success, and so on. Your intuition that complete happiness is possible is correct; you've just been looking in the wrong place, among impermanent phenomena. What you have been looking for all along, intuitively, is the Bodhicitta. When you have that, you have everything. All your desires will be fulfilled by that experience.' Śāntideva, in his *Bodhicāryāvatāra*, compares the extraordinary sense of joy and surprise that accompanies the arising of the Bodhicitta to that of a blind man finding a precious jewel in a dung-heap.[20]

Having found the real wish-fulfilling gem, the experience of Enlightened Compassion, we shall feel totally satisfied. Then all we shall want to do is share with others the limitless spiritual riches we have found. So the first of the Perfections – the main spiritual practices of someone in whom the Bodhicitta has arisen – is generosity. He or she is prepared to give anything to help others.

In some Tantric initiations, those receiving the initiation take the 'pledge of Ratnasambhava'. This is a promise always to give material goods, friendship, fearlessness, and the Dharma to whoever needs them. Some Bodhisattvas have given up everything they had, even life and limb, to help others. At the same time, generosity and altruism, even on this scale, are not seen as terrible ordeals. The Bodhisattva's work for the world is described as *līlā* – 'playfulness'! This is because the Bodhisattva, in whom the Bodhicitta has arisen, does not become caught up with things. Everything he or she does is easy and spontaneous. The Bodhisattva lives permanently within the 'greater mandala', dwells all the time in the mandala of the five Buddhas. He or she is constantly in touch with Ratnasambhava, living in his Pure Land.

This Pure Land, where Ratnasambhava's Wisdom reigns supreme, has all the characteristics of the Golden Age described in myth and poetry. Its inhabitants are prosperous, for they can draw endlessly on Ratnasambhava's spiritual riches. They are an equal society, for all divisive distinctions have melted away in his golden light. They are innocent of selfishness and the craving and hatred that it breeds. They are playful, with the constant spontaneity of the Bodhisattva. They are creative both artistically and spiritually, as they fashion their surroundings and their minds into ever more pleasing forms.

To enter that Pure Land, the Glorious, you just have to look into Akṣobhya's impassive mirror. As you carefully watch the procession of life forms reflected within it, including yourself, you will come to understand that in their depths they are all the same. Then you will no longer fear letting go of your boundary, in case what you have should disappear. You will not hold back from giving lest you are left with nothing. You will happily give yourself completely. Then you will find that you have gained the whole world. You will have inherited the inexhaustible riches of Ratnasambhava.

Amitābha

Eight

The Red Buddha and the Mudrā of Meditation

To enter the next realm we have to follow the sun as it sinks into the west, where lies the land of the red Buddha Amitābha, whose name means 'infinite light'. Here we shall find a great red palace, made of rubies, with a triangular gate. This building has nothing of the powerful fortress-like vajra-defences of Akṣobhya's palace. Nor is it the golden temple of art of Ratnasambhava. The palace of the west is warm and inviting. It is an open, friendly place where you can completely relax.

Above all, it is a magic palace. Within its ruby walls you can have everything you long for. After your long travels you might be famished and a bit bedraggled. If you want food, it will magically appear. New clothes? You have only to think of them to find yourself wearing them.

Before we explore the western realm more thoroughly, though, it has to be said that we do not have to make a long journey to get there. According to the Pure Land schools of Mahāyāna Buddhism, there is a much easier way. These schools base their doctrine on certain sūtras that concern Amitābha, and how he came to achieve Buddhahood.

According to the Mahāyāna, in order to gain total Enlightenment you first have to follow the path of the Bodhisattva. A Bodhisattva, we have seen, is someone who has vowed to gain Enlightenment for the sake of all living beings, to help them gain the happiness of nirvāṇa in their turn. So the practice of Bodhisattvas is essentially altruistic: they pursue their spiritual development in order to become a greater resource on which other beings can draw. In the course of aeons of spiritual practice, they

97

give whatever they can to living beings, helping them in every way imaginable (and, as they become spiritually advanced, in ways that it is hard for us to imagine at all).

A Bodhisattva sets out on this path to Enlightenment by taking a number of public vows. It is said, in the *Larger Sukhāvatī Vyūha Sūtra*, that aeons ago there was a young man called Dharmākara, who vowed to gain Enlightenment in the presence of a Buddha called Lokeśvararāja. In fact, he made forty-eight great vows, all aimed at benefiting living beings. The eighteenth of these was especially important.

> When I have attained Buddhahood, if those beings who are in the ten quarters should believe in me with serene thoughts, and should wish to be born in my country, and should have, say, ten times thought of me (or repeated my name) – if they should not be born there, may I not obtain the perfect knowledge; – barring only those who have committed the five heinous crimes, and those who have spoken ill of the good Dharma.[21]

Through this vow, Dharmākara made it a condition of his obtaining Buddhahood that he would be able to create a Pure Land in which almost anyone who had been devoted to him, even slightly, could be reborn. Later in the *Larger Sukhāvatī Vyūha Sūtra*, Śākyamuni Buddha tells his attendant Ānanda that Dharmākara has since become a Buddha, named Amitābha, and has created a Pure Land called Sukhāvatī ('happy land', Tibetan *Dewachen*). As Dharmākara made his attainment of Enlightenment conditional on creating a happy land in which his devotees could be reborn, it follows that – as he has gained Buddhahood – he must have fulfilled his vow.

Thus the Pure Land schools of Buddhism consider that there is no need for long journeys or great struggles. It is enough to recite *oṃ namo amitābhāya buddhāya*, or, in Japanese, *namu amida butsu* (homage to the Buddha Amitābha), to enter Amitābha's Pure Land. These schools of Buddhism seem to depend on 'other-power' (Japanese *tariki*) rather than 'self-power' (Japanese *jiriki*). Rather than striving to gain Enlightenment through your own efforts, you rely on being caught by what the *Tibetan Book of the Dead* calls 'the light-ray hook of blessed Amitābha's compassion'. By calling on him, a portion of the infinite merit he has gained in his practice of the Dharma is transferred to you, and you find yourself after death passing on to a totally different environment.

You are in a golden sheath of light. You cannot see out of it. It is as though you have become very small, like a bee or tiny fairy, and ensconced yourself in a golden daffodil. From somewhere outside you can hear the sounds of birds singing, running waters, and tinkling bells. You feel very secure and happy.

Eventually the sheath around you breaks apart. You realize that you have been cradled in the bud of a golden lotus, which has now opened. You gaze around and take in the details of the Happy Land. A great flat plain stretches away in all directions, covered with a forest of trees. The trees are made of jewels, and in them sit colourful birds who sing songs reminding you of the impermanence and insubstantiality of all things. Great rivers flow through the plain, bearing jewelled flowers. The waters, too, make a sound that communicates the depths of the Dharma. From time to time gentle winds blow, causing a rain of flowers to fall from the sky. Everything you could ask for – food, clothing, palaces – appear at your wish. The whole land is permeated by an unimaginable radiance.

In all directions there are vast lotus flowers, upon which sit golden Buddhas teaching the Dharma. In the middle of the whole shining scene is the Buddha Amitābha, seated on a great lotus throne, flanked by his two chief Bodhisattvas, Avalokiteśvara and Mahāsthāmaprāpta. Now you know that you have been reborn in Sukhāvatī, in which conditions are ideal for spiritual progress. You can never fall back into the mundane world, but little by little, bathed in happiness and continuously hearing the Dharma, you will develop until you too have attained supreme and perfect Buddhahood.

The qualities of Amitābha
Of all the archetypal Buddhas known to the Buddhist tradition, Amitābha has the most devotees, and meditation upon him is the most widespread. We have seen that in China and Japan his cult of devotion became a separate school, or collection of schools, a distinction awarded to no other Buddha. Amitābha (Tibetan *Opame*) is hardly less popular in

A Guide to the Buddhas

countries following the Indo-Tibetan tradition. Doubtless his popularity is due partly to the extreme ease with which, according to the *Sukhāvatī Vyūha Sūtras*, devotion to him can lead to Enlightenment.

He is also very attractive because he symbolizes attraction. Although he is sometimes depicted as golden, his normal colour is a deep ruby-red. In Indo-Tibetan Buddhism, red is the colour of love and compassion, and of the whole emotional aspect of life.

Amitābha, then, is the Buddha of Love and Compassion. As such, he is totally approachable. His time of day is sunset, and his direction the west. So he is like the setting sun. Sunset is a miracle; you can look directly into the fierce power of the sun, and it is gentle and causes you no harm. As it disappears into the west the sun is like a proud and fierce king, who at the end of the day's hunting across the sky turns gentle and jovial, and allows anyone to approach him. (Also, the setting sun may suggest the withdrawal of the light of consciousness from the world of the senses as it turns within to higher states of meditative concentration.)

The spiritual power of Amitābha is all warmth and gentleness. He is the colour of rubies. His colour is the most striking, the first colour recognized by children. He is the colour of fascination. He is the colour of blood. He is the blushing colour of delicate emotion, the suffusing shade of emotional arousal. Through him, all one's emotional energy is led gently into the quest for Enlightenment.

The poison (Sanskrit *kleśa*) with which he is associated is *rāga* – passion. The nature of passion is that it attaches itself strongly to a particular object. The practice of the Amitābha sādhana arouses emotional energy, but transmutes mundane passion into Discriminating Wisdom. This is the counterbalance to the Wisdom of Equality of Ratnasambhava, which saw the common factor in all changing appearances. The Wisdom of Amitābha sees the uniqueness, the distinctive characteristics, of every phenomenon.

A passionate lover wants just to be with the one unique, seemingly irreplaceable, person who is the object of their love. They are highly aware of that person's distinctive qualities. Small things about them are endearing: a particular mannerism, a way of moving the head, a typical phrase.

100

All these are special and lovable because they are signs, distinguishing marks, of the loved one. Similarly, the Discriminating Wisdom of Amitābha sees and loves the minute differences in things. The distinction between the lover's appreciation and Amitābha's Wisdom is that Discriminating Wisdom is non-dual. It introduces no idea of self and other. Hence it does not make its loving appreciation of uniqueness into a basis for exclusive attachment.

The Lotus family

Amitābha's special emblem is the lotus, and he is head of the Lotus (Sanskrit *Padma*) family. He is thus associated with all the attributes of the lotus: gentleness, openness, and the more 'receptive' qualities. The quality of openness is further stressed by his element, fire, which consumes everything, creating space. Even more so, the totality of his openness is reflected in a legend associated with his heraldic animal, the peacock. According to myth, peacocks are capable of swallowing poisonous snakes without coming to harm. This symbolism, of being open even to poison, and transmuting it into beauty (as the snake nourishes the peacock's beautiful plumage) is very striking. It gives us a feeling for the transforming power of Amitābha's love and compassion. On an everyday level, this legend suggests that even our darkest and most venomous aspects can be transformed by practising the Dharma.

The realm of the Wheel of Life which Amitābha transmutes is that of the hungry ghosts. These are beings whose lives are spent in frustrated craving. They are usually portrayed with large stomachs and tiny mouths. Amitābha's love dissolves away the feelings of desperation and being unloved and unlovable that cause them to grab at life. His power of meditation takes them away from their restless and unfulfilled state onto a deeper and more satisfying level of themselves.

In general, the path to Enlightenment represented by Amitābha is the reverse of Akṣobhya's. The approach of the Vajra family is more overtly dynamic. Through it you become increasingly vajric, breaking through obstacles, hurtling towards Enlightenment. The approach of Amitābha is more 'organic'. Gently and gradually you unfold the petals of your spiritual potential until you ripen into Enlightenment. The path of

Akṣobhya, transmuting hatred, is one of aversion to saṃsāra, the restless urge to break free from its chains. Amitābha's path is one of attraction to nirvāṇa, the longing desire to embrace that warm red sun.

As Amitābha has attracted so much devotion, many of the most well known and important figures in Buddhist tradition are naturally members of his Lotus family. I shall do no more than mention some of them here, as many are fully discussed in the second and third books in this series. They include Avalokiteśvara, White Tārā, Padmasambhava, Hayagrīva, and Padmanarteśvara (lotus lord of dance), as well as Śākyamuni, whom we have already met.

Amitābha also has a reflex form – Amitāyus.[22] *Āyus* means life in Sanskrit, so Amitāyus is infinite life. He is particularly associated with practices for gaining longevity. While Amitābha is usually represented holding a begging bowl, Amitāyus holds a precious vase, full of the nectar of immortality. The two figures 'Infinite Light' and 'Infinite Life' clearly represent the same principle from the point of view of space and time respectively. Indeed, Indian Buddhism seems to treat Amitābha and Amitāyus as the same figure, and it is only in the Tantric Buddhism of Tibet and Japan that one finds them regarded as separate.

As befits his popularity, there are many meditations associated with Amitābha. As we have seen, in the Pure Land schools the simple repetition of his mantra is highly recommended. Some schools hold that the power of Amitābha's vow is so great that they deem it unnecessary even to recite the mantra in order to be reborn in Sukhāvatī. Rather, they take the view that one should recite it simply as an expression of gratitude to Amitābha for certain rebirth in his Pure Land. To practise in such a way obviously requires a tremendous amount of faith.

This discussion of 'other-power' and the saving vow of Amitābha may sound similar to the 'saving grace' of God in Christianity. We do not have space here to discuss this in detail; I shall just make a few points. Firstly, nowhere is there any suggestion that Amitābha is a creator God. He is represented as gaining Enlightenment through his own efforts, and other beings can attain the same Enlightened state as him. Secondly, as we saw in Chapter Three, Buddhism denies any ultimate distinction between self and other, so terms such as 'other-power' or 'self-reliance' pertain only to the level of relative truth.

There is also perhaps a more sophisticated way of understanding the Pure Land tradition. According to this, Sukhāvatī with its wonders is essentially a colourful symbol for Enlightenment. People who see it in this way are likely to be sceptical of the claim that repetition of Amitābha's name while in an ordinary state of consciousness could bring about one's escape from saṃsāra. For them, one would aim to arrive at a state of pure devotion to Amitābha, through repetition of the mantra, without even the slightest admixture of self-concern. It would be such 'moments of egolessness' that would provide the real passport to insight into Reality, symbolized by birth in Amitābha's Pure Land.

Amitābha visualizations

Although simple recitation of the mantra is considered by the Pure Land schools sufficient means to reach Sukhāvatī, we saw in Chapter Two that there is a Pure Land scripture that gives a very detailed series of meditation exercises in which one can gradually build up an imaginative vision of Sukhāvatī. These fourteen meditations are given in the *Amitāyur Dhyāna Sūtra*. They begin with a meditation on the orb of the setting sun. From there they proceed through contemplation of the features of the Pure Land (e.g. giving a very detailed and complex description of the phantasmagoria of jewel trees, jewel lakes, and so on), and culminate in the contemplation of the brilliant figures of the Buddha Amitāyus and his attendant Bodhisattvas. All this interwoven beauty and proliferation of riches has to be visualized repeatedly, until the whole scene appears clearly, whether your eyes are closed or open. To dwell constantly on the Pure Land in this way has an extraordinary effect on the mind. Devotedly practising the meditations one comes to dwell more and more in Sukhāvatī, to feel oneself in the presence of Amitāyus in this very life.

Similar meditations appear in the Tibetan tradition. For instance, there is a 'sādhana of Dewachen' associated with the lama Minjur Dorje. This is a quite complex meditation, involving the making of many rich offerings to Amitābha, before finally identifying oneself with him (at which point 'self-power' and 'other-power' become one). There are also various yogas of 'transference of consciousness' (Tibetan *phowa*) involving Amitābha, whose aim is to enable one to gain Enlightenment at the moment of death or, failing that, to transfer one's consciousness to Amitābha's Pure Land. In addition, there are a number of Amitāyus yogas, aimed at producing long life. In Tibetan sādhanas, the mantra of Amitābha is usually *oṃ amideva hrīḥ*.

While he may be golden, as we have seen, in most sādhanas Amitābha is a glowing warm red, with curly blue-black hair. He is always seated in the full-lotus posture of meditation, and generally his hands are in the dhyāna mudrā, though occasionally he may be holding up a red lotus in his right hand. He is dressed in ornately embroidered deep-red robes. Around his head there is usually a glowing green aura, and around his body a red one. Both are edged with rainbows.

Sometimes he is visualized seated on a deep-red lotus which floats on a calm ocean, so that his radiant form – like a setting sun – casts a path of light across the waters. Through regularly performing a sādhana such as this, we can absorb the glowing warmth of love and compassion that radiates from Amitābha. Our minds gradually acquire something of his oceanic depth of feeling. We become like the great ocean, with a warm centre of unfailing love at our hearts. The restless waves of thought all stilled, our meditation takes on something of the deep tranquillity of the meditating figure we are visualizing. For many people, the visualization of Amitābha is particularly approachable. His warm power is endlessly attractive and his figure is simple, symmetrical, and easy to visualize.

The meditating Buddha

Though it is simple, Amitābha's figure has an archetypal quality to it. He is a meditating Buddha, with his hands in the dhyāna mudrā – the mudrā of meditation. When people without any special interest in it think about Buddhism, it is this image that frequently comes to mind. The meditating Buddha can now be found in many places in the West: in museums and galleries, in books and in junk shops. (I have even seen one turned into a lampstand.)

The meditating Buddha is the central image of Buddhism, arising out of the crucial experience of the entire Buddhist tradition: the Buddha's attainment of Enlightenment while seated in deep meditation under the bodhi tree. As we saw in Chapter Six, before the Buddha answered his challenge by calling the Earth Goddess to witness, Māra had tried much cruder tactics. He had sent against the meditating Buddha a great army of misshapen demons who hurled rocks, spears, and all manner of other weapons. However, the Buddha never opened his eyes, but silently continued his meditation. The arrows, javelins, and so forth showered down about him, but as they touched the aura of light surrounding his body they were transformed into flowers and fell in a gentle rain around his peaceful figure. Māra then sent his three daughters to beguile and seduce him. The Buddha did not so much as glance at them, but just carried on his inward quest for freedom.

One should be able to tell a great deal about a spiritual tradition just by contemplating its central symbol. Surprisingly, I think this is particularly true if you just contemplate the image, without any explanation of its supposed meaning within the tradition. (For example, contemplating a crucifix, purely as an image, can tell you a great deal about the nature of Christianity.) The meditating Buddha, the central symbol of Buddhism, is, I think, part of the reason why Buddhism enjoys a good reputation in the West. People are often well-disposed to Buddhism because, without their necessarily being very conscious of it, the meditating Buddha image has deeply affected them.

If you look at a meditating Buddha figure, in stone, bronze, brass, plaster, wood, or whatever, you pick up certain impressions. Its posture is regular, well-balanced, pleasing. It has a solidity about it. It is upright and immovable. It doesn't worry or bite its nails. It is centred. In fact it looks almost as though it had put down roots into the earth.

The figure just sits, silent, contented. He has no appointments to make, no train to catch. He is peaceful, calm, welcoming. If you have a few minutes to sit with him and join him in meditation, before you have to rush off, he will be pleased.

He is timeless. He could sit there for ever. Some of the old stone Buddhas seem to have been sitting silently, deepening their concentration, for a thousand years or more. The Buddhas at Nālandā in India have meditated steadily through changing fortunes. First covered in garlands and cared for by devoted monks, then suffering patiently as Muslim invaders beat at them with sticks, now they are still rapt in concentration while planes fly overhead and tourists wander by.

There is something awe-inspiring about a meditating Buddha. What is he gazing at deep within, with that faint smile of knowledge on his lips? One feels he has dived into an endless inner ocean, to find the sunken treasures of the universe, the rubies of the mind.

A figure in the meditation posture can be awe-inspiring whether made of stone or flesh and blood. A story is told of Daito, a Zen master, who for a while lived with beggars under the bridges of Kyoto. In those days it was the brutal custom for a samurai to test a new sword on a human victim. One evening a samurai was seen roaming the area with a new sword. The beggars were terrified as they knew that after dark the samurai would come to test his sword on one of their 'expendable' number. Daito told them all to hide. Then he sat himself calmly in the meditation posture on the road. Night fell. The samurai came along, and saw an unmoving victim. He cried out to Daito to prepare to die, as he was going to cleave him in two with his sword. There was no reply. The calm figure sat in front of him, giving off that feeling of vast, gently harnessed energy which comes from someone in deep meditation. Looking at his serene victim, the samurai faltered, unnerved. Finally he slunk away into the night.[23]

The mudrā of meditation

Let us come back to Amitābha, our meditating Buddha. Look at his hands. They are joined, one hand resting on the other, thumbs lightly touching, placed near the centre of his body. What can they tell us? They speak of how relaxed he is. They express the union of opposites. They are both active and receptive. The thumbs just touch. With less exertion they would not meet, with more they would press upwards and break the perfect oval formed by the hands. They are suggestive of the Middle Way and the Buddha's advice to Soṇa. Soṇa was a monk who practised walking meditation for so long, pacing up and down, that his feet bled. The Buddha explained to him how in his meditation he should be like a well-tuned lute. If the strings are either too slack or too tight it cannot be played. The gently-touching thumbs maintain a constant awareness of a balanced spiritual development.

We have looked at the hands, but we have yet to consider the most important aspect of the mudrā. What we have not looked at is the oval space enclosed between the palms and the arch of the thumbs. Amitābha, like all meditating Buddhas, embraces space as his most precious possession. That oval space is like an egg, like the egg of Emptiness at the centre of the vajra. The meditating Buddha sits patiently 'incubating' this egg of space. What will be hatched from it? A Buddha's only concern is to create conditions that will be helpful for living beings to escape from suffering. So from the egg of Emptiness an entire Pure Land will emerge, with its jewel trees and lotuses, its infinite radiances and inexhaustible Dharma teachings.

It is through the power of his meditation on infinite love and compassion that Amitābha brings his Pure Land into existence. However, even love and compassion would not be enough to create this greatest of all masterpieces of the mind. It is only when combined with an understanding of Emptiness, of the insubstantial nature of all phenomena, that Amitābha's feelings for all beings can create a world for them to live in, in which they can make steady progress towards complete happiness.

Watching Amitābha creating a Pure Land through his mental power should raise a question in our minds. If a Buddha creates a mental world, is the situation any different for ordinary beings such as us? The general answer of Buddhism seems to be that we, too, are creating our world all the time – not a Pure Land, but a world that is pure or impure depending on the skilfulness, or unskilfulness, of our volitions.

We create a world, but all too often, like bored factory hands on a production line, we constantly churn out the same old product, the same shoddy goods. We have become so numbed to the whole process that we do it without thinking. We could do it in our sleep (and we do: even in sleep we create worlds for ourselves, but dismiss them as mere dreams). Most of the time, the production line goes too fast for us to alter the kind of world that we produce. We are usually too numbed or distracted to see the process at work. So we cannot understand what has gone wrong when, through blind aversion and reaction, we build ourselves a hell to live in. Nor do we realize that, with a fresh plan and some work, we could create our own Pure Land.

To see how we can set about this, we have to go back to contemplating our meditating Buddha, back to Amitābha. We have to learn the lesson of that oval of space which he caresses in the dhyāna mudrā. It is through the spacious awareness which we can create in meditation, space to look at how our thoughts create a world, that we can change *our* world.

Contemplating the serene figure of Amitābha, meditating among the jewel trees of his western realm, we can understand more clearly what is at stake in meditation practice. Through meditation we can come to see that we do create our world, and begin to take responsibility for it. In meditation we make the aware space in which we look at the world we are creating, and then work to create a new world for ourselves by raising our level of consciousness.

Through meditation, rather than being bored, resentful factory hands, we can become master craftsmen, lovingly shaping our world. We can continue this meditative process indefinitely, creating worlds of greater and greater happiness and beauty. Finally, we too will be able to sit like Amitābha, silent and still as a great mountain yet vastly energetic, incubating that egg of Emptiness within our hands. As our meditation on love and compassion becomes infinitely deep, from that empty space will begin to pour a whole world. Rivers will flow from it, adorned with jewelled lotuses. Colourful birds will fly out, singing of the Dharma. Then a deep-red lotus bud will appear, tightly closed. As the warm rays of love from our hearts fall upon it, the lotus will slowly unfold, and we shall see all beings cradled, safe at last, in the empty space between our hands.

Amoghasiddhi

Nine

Crossed Thunderbolts and the Buddha of Action

After the last delicate rays of the setting sun have tinted the sky, night falls. You make your final journey, completing your circuit of the mandala, into the north, a country of green pine forests. It is dark as you walk between the huge trees. In the forest you can hear rustlings and cries. It would be easy to become afraid, and turn back, but if you were to do so you would never meet Amoghasiddhi, the Buddha of the northern realm, whose name means 'unobstructed success'.

You walk for hours, with the whispering wings of owls overhead. Finally, at midnight, you emerge from the forest into a clearing. Ahead of you is a palace made entirely of jade and emerald. It towers into the air, vertical, a mass of roofs and pinnacles. You go forward eagerly, then stop. There is a gate to the palace, yes. It is in the shape of a great bow, string uppermost. However, the gate is set high up in the smooth wall. Only an eagle could enter such a gate.

As you stand, not knowing what to do, you hear a great commotion from within the palace: rhythmic crashings. Suddenly the bow-shaped gate lifts high and, like an arrow shot by a giant, something flies forth from the palace. It is a chariot, drawn by two strange figures. At first they look like eagles, with wings and talons. Then you see that their hands and torsos are human. In their hands they each hold a huge pair of cymbals, which they clash together as they fly.

On the chariot, seated on a green lotus seat, is a dark green Buddha, clad in scarlet robes. The light from his body transforms the midnight scene so that everything is radiant and clear. His right hand is raised in a power-ful gesture, which seems to banish the darkness and fears of the night. In his left hand sits a mysterious emblem: two diamond thunderbolts crossed and fused together.

He hurtles effortlessly above you. As he does so, the huge pines are trans-formed into a forest of jewel trees. Has the green Buddha ridden out of his palace, or into it? Can you have been in his Pure Land all along, with-out realizing it?

Of all Buddha figures, Amoghasiddhi (Tibetan *Donyo Drup pa*) is per-haps the most mysterious and ungraspable. His attributes and emblems are redolent of power and energy, yet his activity is subtle and hidden. These qualities are clearly shown in the beginning of a sādhana of Amoghasiddhi. First, as usual, appears the vast expanse of the sky, sym-bol of the empty and insubstantial nature of all phenomena. However, in the case of Amoghasiddhi, this sky is not the rich blue of the sky lit by sunlight – the bright warm blue of the Spanish sun above my head as I write. The sky of Amoghasiddhi is the deep velvet blue of midnight in the tropics.

Then, in the depths of the midnight sky, there appears a gigantic double vajra. The two diamond thunderbolts are crossed, and made of pure crystal. As we saw when we met Akṣobhya, the single vajra is a symbol of awesome power and force. It can cut through anything while always remaining unaffected. Nothing mundane can withstand its impact. The double vajra has all these qualities reinforced.

The double vajra is a symbol of total psychic integration, of the unfold-ment of all potential, of perfect harmony, balance, and equilibrium. It can only be encountered when one has journeyed into the most pro-found depths of existence. It can only appear out of the midnight sky of the deepest unconscious. Visualizing it against the deep-blue sky, one feels it to be the primordial pattern of human consciousness. It is the per-fect ground plan, the potential which we try falteringly and semi-consciously to unfold in our lives.

Not only is it the ground, the blueprint, for human consciousness, it is also, according to Indian Buddhist cosmology, the support on which the universe rests. Buddhist cosmology has a vision every bit as expansive as modern astronomy. It sees universes evolving and passing out of existence over the aeons. The entire universe with its world systems is said to have as its foundation an inconceivably large double vajra.

It has been suggested that this vision of the basis of the cosmos being a double vajra could even have been an attempt to describe something of the same vision of the universe as that of modern science. If you were a Buddhist yogin or yogini, and in the depths of your meditation you went beyond the individual to the universal, and witnessed the passing of aeons, with galaxies appearing and disappearing, how could you describe it? Buddhist cosmology has managed to do it, in terms that we can recognize.

Then what if your mind encompassed even the birth of the universe, the big bang that precipitated our cosmos into being? How could you describe that unthinkable explosion? Perhaps the nearest description you could find would be that the whole universe was founded on a vast double thunderbolt, its energies pouring outward from a central point.

Regardless of whether or not the double vajra has any connection with the big bang, we can draw a profound lesson from its symbolism. The double vajra supports the universe. It also forms the deepest pattern in the midnight depths of our own psyche. So the fundamental matrix of both the universe and of every individual consciousness within it is the same. In their common depths, the individual and the universal interpenetrate. To understand yourself, in your deepest nature, is to understand the nature of the universe.

Thus the symbolism of the double vajra suggests the interpenetration, even the fusion, of different levels of existence. In it, thunderbolts intersect, diamond cuts diamond and they fuse together. In the double vajra all opposites unite. With this interpenetration and union of opposites comes total psychic balance, and integration.

The symbolism of the union of opposites extends beyond the double vajra into Amoghasiddhi's other attributes. As we saw, he is pulled through space by strange winged creatures. In Indian Buddhism the animals of Amoghasiddhi are usually garuḍas (Tibetan *khyung po*) –

mythical royal birds, enemies of the serpent-like *nāgas*. However, in Tibetan iconography the garuḍas transformed themselves into *shang-shang* creatures – half man, half bird – a fusion of human and animal. Lama Govinda says of Amoghasiddhi,

> This Inner Way leads into the mystery of Amoghasiddhi: in which the inner and the outer world, the visible and the invisible, are united; and in which the spiritual takes bodily shape, and the body becomes an exponent of the spirit. For Amoghasiddhi is the lord of the great transformation, whose vehicle is the winged man, the man in transition towards a new dimension of consciousness.[24]

Not only are the shang-shang birds themselves a union of opposites, but as they fly through space they clash together cymbals, forcibly uniting all poles of existence.

The symbolism of hybrid creatures is quite a common one in Buddhism. According to legend, for a short period after the time of Śākyamuni Buddha's Enlightenment, all hatred in the world ceased. During that time, animals who were natural foes mated to produce animals with qualities which are antipathetic in the natural world.

It is this fusion of opposites which gives Amoghasiddhi his mysterious quality. It is really only possible to speak of him in the language of paradox and contradiction. As we shall see, he is particularly associated with energy and action, yet that action is based on the completeness of the double vajra, which leaves no feeling of a need to act, no volition. He is, in a sense, the most active and outward-going of the five Buddhas (e.g. he is associated with the five sense-consciousnesses, which apprehend the external world), yet his activity springs from the encounter with the double vajra in the innermost depths of consciousness.

Thus the effects of meditating on Amoghasiddhi seem to be subtle and hard to grasp. You may not notice much external change for a while, yet deep down in your being the energies of your psyche are being led into the harmonious patterning called forth by the double vajra. This acts as a form of mandala which, as we saw in Chapter Five, tends to order our energies like iron filings around a magnet. Deep conflicts begin to resolve. Energy is released, but as from a secret spring.

In performing the practice you may come to see the world in a more complex, less one-sided way. You begin to understand the practical paradoxes of the spiritual life. You see that to help others is to help yourself. You cannot develop spiritually yourself without helping others to do so. Also, to complete any aspect of development is to begin a new phase. You cannot develop true wisdom without compassion, or vice versa. But, above all else, Amoghasiddhi gradually shows you how self and other, individual and universal, fuse in the diamond-hard centre of the double thunderbolt.

Amoghasiddhi as embodiment of fearlessness

One of the most striking things about the figure of Amoghasiddhi is the power of the gesture he makes with his right hand. It is turned outwards, at the level of his heart, fingers pointing skyward. It is a gesture of command and authority, the *abhaya* mudrā or 'gesture of fearlessness'. Amoghasiddhi's whole presence removes terror and fear. His body is green, the colour of the peace and tranquillity of Nature. Green is soothing and relaxing, and calms anxiety.

We have seen that each of the five Buddhas may have been contacted through deep meditation on the life of Śākyamuni Buddha. According to tradition,[25] shortly after his Enlightenment, while he was still staying by the banks of the River Nerañjarā, there arose a tremendous rainstorm, which lasted for seven days. During the storm the Buddha was protected by the nāga-king Mucalinda, who coiled around him and spread his hood over the Buddha's head to protect him. This incident seems to represent the final stage of the Enlightenment process, during which the Buddha assimilated what he had seen, allowing his insight into the nature of things to permeate all the levels of his being. Amoghasiddhi, as bearer of the crossed vajras, stresses the total nature of the Enlightenment experience, transforming all aspects of oneself. Interestingly, Amoghasiddhi is sometimes represented with a canopy of snakes above his head.[26]

Apart from this, it is easy to find examples of fearlessness in Śākyamuni's life which could have led people to Amoghasiddhi. There was once a time when threats had been made on the Buddha's life. During the night he emerged from his hut to find monks with sticks standing guard to protect him. He just told them 'a Buddha needs no protection,' and sent them away.

On another occasion, the Buddha's cousin, Devadatta, in a fit of jealousy, bribed someone to let loose a wild elephant against the Buddha. We can imagine the scene: people scattering in all directions; Devadatta perhaps hidden somewhere out of harm's way where he could watch events; the great beast rushing, maddened, towards the one still figure in a mud-dyed ochre robe. It is an extraordinary contrast. The elephant out of control, head tossing, trunk waving, furious; the Buddha still, erect, serene.

As the beast came towards him, the Buddha suffused it with *maitrī*, loving-kindness. Nothing could have entered that enchanted circle of love around the Buddha and maintained thoughts of violence. The mad elephant discovered it was bearing down on the best friend it had in the world. Gradually its charge slowed to a walk, and it reached the Buddha docile and friendly. In this incident we could say that elephant met elephant, for the Buddha was often described as being like a great elephant because of his calm dignity and steady gaze. Perhaps elephant met elephant in a deeper sense too. The Buddha, having gone far beyond dualistic modes of thought, did not feel himself a separate, threatened identity opposed by the huge creature bearing down upon him. His *maitrī* came from a total feeling for, and identification with, the charging animal.

The previous incidents show the Buddha dealing fearlessly with trouble coming his way, but on some occasions the Buddha deliberately put himself in perilous situations in order to help people. Perhaps the best known example of this is to be found in the story of Aṅgulimāla, whose name means 'garland of fingers'. Aṅgulimāla had taken a vow to kill a hundred people. From each victim he hacked a finger and added it to a gruesome necklace. At the time of the Buddha's arrival in the vicinity, Aṅgulimāla's finger total had nearly reached a hundred. He was ferocious, and had terrorized the whole area. No one could withstand him. The Buddha was given a solemn warning about travelling into his domain. He immediately took a route that would bring him close to the assassin's lair.

Aṅgulimāla saw the figure of the monk walking quietly along, reached for his sword, and rushed after the Buddha. However, although he was fit and strong, and was running full pelt while the Buddha was mindfully walking, Aṅgulimāla could not catch him up. He redoubled his efforts, but still the steady paces outdistanced him.

Finally, exhausted and baffled, Aṅgulimāla cried out 'Stop monk!' The Buddha's calm reply was, 'I have stopped, Aṅgulimāla.' The Buddha's mind had stopped dealing in craving, hatred, and ignorance, and had arrived at a place which Aṅgulimāla could not reach with his sword. Aṅgulimāla was so impressed that he went for Refuge, becoming a disciple of the Buddha.

This last incident contains several echoes of the symbolism of Amoghasiddhi. There is the fearlessness of the Buddha, there is his active approach in going to find Aṅgulimāla, there is the mystery and paradox of how the Buddha, sauntering, always outdistances the rushing cutthroat. Amoghasiddhi can show us how true fearlessness is to be attained. Ultimately it can come only from insight into Reality. At that point we realize the illusoriness of the ego which we fear for. In particular, fear of dying, the primary fear of which all others are reflections, disappears. There is no one to die.

The double vajra reminds us that fearlessness comes from a full and balanced development of all sides of ourselves. Without that, we shall always have a weak side, a vulnerability that we fear for and keep having to protect. Even more, we shall have an unexplored aspect, an area of uncharted terrain within, whose characteristics we may experience, projected onto the outside world, as people and situations that are unpredictable and threatening.

It is all too easy to keep developing one's strengths, and to try to make use of them in all situations. Some people even manage to become totally identified with a single talent or a powerful position. From a spiritual point of view this is dangerous. If you wanted to defend a castle, you would not work to make just one or two sides impregnable. Following the Dharma involves developing all aspects of character, all spiritual qualities.

Our aim must be to become the double vajra. One way of checking whether our development is proceeding in this harmonious way is to consider the teaching of the five *indriyas* or 'spiritual faculties'. These are: confidence and trust in the Three Jewels, wisdom, concentration, energy, and mindfulness. They can be arranged in a mandala pattern, with two balanced pairs and a central faculty. You could imagine each of the pairs corresponding to a vajra of the double vajra. In this way you have confidence in the west, wisdom in the east, concentration in the south, and energy in the north. The central point, from which all the faculties grow, and which assures their balanced development, is mindfulness or awareness.

The path of Amoghasiddhi, then, is a path of overcoming fear. Performing his sādhana involves courageously diving into the midnight depths of ourselves, finding there the blueprint of our potential, and being prepared to work on the weakest and most embryonic aspects of ourselves. Finally, as we shall see in the next section, it will mean going out bravely into the world to take the Dharma to others. This is no easy path to follow, but if we take up the challenge, then, all the time we are working to overcome our fears, the calm, dark-green figure of a Buddha will stand by our side, his right hand extended in that unanswerable gesture of fearlessness, bestowing on us the courage and confidence to follow that path to the end.

Spontaneous action and unobstructed success

Several years ago a young man who suffered from epilepsy asked a Buddhist teacher to choose a visualization practice for him. The guru suggested he meditate on Amoghasiddhi, saying that an epileptic fit seemed to involve a discharge of excess energy. As it was a particularly high-energy meditation, the Amoghasiddhi sādhana could help to absorb that excess energy.

Amoghasiddhi is the Buddha of action. The green Buddha does not sit on a calm ocean like Amitābha. Instead, he is pulled through space by his bird-men, rushing onwards, to the stirring clash of their cymbals. His main emblem is the double vajra which must, in a sense, represent even greater harnessed energy than the single one, for it has added another dimension. It is energy completely freed, capable of moving in any direction or in all directions at once.

It is for this reason that Amoghasiddhi is associated with the element air, and with sound, which moves out in all directions. In Tantric symbolism the air element is related to the throat chakra, which is concerned with communication. The quality of the sound produced when people speak is usually a very good indicator of their energy level.

The activity of Amoghasiddhi is spontaneous and altruistic. He moves out into the world as an expression of the compassionate heart of all the Buddhas. He and Amitābha form a complementary pair. While Amitābha's compassionate influence is brought to bear on the world from the depths of meditation, Amoghasiddhi makes that influence tangible and visible. He could be said to represent *upāya*, the 'skilful means' by which Enlightened beings attract people to the Dharma. A Buddha or advanced Bodhisattva will have myriad ways of leading people away from saṃsāra and onto the spiritual path. They will adopt any form, any mode of behaviour, necessary to put people in touch with the Dharma.

Another of Amoghasiddhi's connections is with volition – the will to act. It is volitions which create karma. We move towards some things and people, and away from (or against) others. This constant mental movement produces consequences. As we saw in the previous chapter, each of us creates a world in which to live, and it is through our volitions (Sanskrit *saṃskāras*) that we do this. If we are to 'stop the world' and get off the wheel of rebirth and suffering, our task is to prevent these volitions arising. As long as we are still emotionally entangled with the world, trying to force situations to continue or to disappear, our relationship with it will continue, and we shall not be free.

An Enlightened person produces no volitions in the ordinary sense at all. Seeing everything mundane as being like a reflection or a dream, he or she no longer moves towards it or away from it. If you were given a hundred gold bars, you would probably be elated. If someone tried to hit you, you might be angry or afraid. However, if when these things happened you knew that you were dreaming, you would no longer be affected by them. Knowing the true nature of the situation, you could give away the gold, or let yourself be hit, with perfect equanimity. So an Enlightened person acts, but without any egotistical volition. Thus their actions are described in Sanskrit as *akarya* – creating no new karma.

As mundane volitions arise from a perceived split between subject and object, they are always divided against themselves. Energy is wasted in the friction between 'self' and 'other', or projected 'out there' and is no longer available to us.

After Enlightenment, the picture changes completely. Once the subject–object duality is seen as illusory, projection dies away. There is no longer any friction or dissipation of energy. It is this state that Amoghasiddhi embodies. He represents action that is total and spontaneous. Total action is perfectly satisfying, because we act with the whole of our being, with nothing left out. When Amoghasiddhi acts, all he does expresses the depth of his being. Every move he makes is sealed with the mark of the double vajra. Action of this totality, with every ounce of the liberated energy of an Enlightened consciousness behind it, is unstoppable. Amoghasiddhi's name – 'unobstructed success' – evokes the inevitable outcome of total action.

Amoghasiddhi's compassionate activity is spontaneous. He does not have to stop to work out the best course of action, or who to help next. All his actions flow unpremeditated, arising naturally out of his panoramic awareness of situations.

It is this unpremeditated altruism which is born from the Wisdom of Amoghasiddhi, known as the All-Accomplishing Wisdom. The spiritual poison that he transmutes into this Wisdom is envy, that most barren and fruitless of feelings. We have seen how Amoghasiddhi's symbolism is concerned with the union of opposites. Fittingly, envy manages to unite craving with hatred or resentment. Envy wishes to succeed, but its eyes are on the external world and the accomplishments of others. Amoghasiddhi teaches us to look within, to mobilize our own resources. If we look deeply enough, we will see the illusory nature of self and other. Envy then becomes equanimity.

Amoghasiddhi presides over the realm of the titans, or *asuras*. These are represented in the Wheel of Life as powerful, jealous beings, always in contention with the gods. To employ stereotypes, they are the career politicians of our world, the young executives prepared to do anything for a directorship. They are energetic and powerful. They despise weakness. The only things they respect are power, energy, money, and success. It is no good giving them sermons on gentleness and humility. They will assume that you are someone weak trying to trick them into giving up their superiority. Anyway, they will probably not even stop to take in your arguments. In the time they spent listening to you, one of their rivals might get ahead of them.

To convert asuras to the Dharma, they need to see that you have something which they do not. Only if you can match their energy and resourcefulness will you get a hearing. Aṅgulimāla listened to the Buddha only when the Buddha had proved to have powers far beyond his own.

For dealing with asuras, Amoghasiddhi has all the power of the crossed vajras, all the energy of total action. Asuras worship success, and his success is unobstructed and infallible. Fearless, developed in a balanced way, without a weakness for the asuras to exploit, he cannot be defeated. He is someone to whom they are prepared to listen, an ideal they can recognize. The dark green Buddha is a figure that even the jealous and suspicious heart of a titan can learn to love.

The followers of Amoghasiddhi, and a nasty fall

Like Ratnasambhava, Amoghasiddhi's cult of devotion never developed very strongly in the East. His Karma – or Action – family encompasses a relatively small number of figures. By far the most important of these is Green Tārā, a lovely female Bodhisattva. The main male Bodhisattva of the Karma family is Viśvapāṇi (holder of everything). He has not gained much prominence in Buddhism, and is hardly ever represented separately from his appearance as an attendant upon Amoghasiddhi.

Though Amoghasiddhi never gathered a large following in the East, he is attracting devotees in the West. Of the Dharma practitioners with whom I am in contact, a significant proportion have taken up the sādhana of Amoghasiddhi, visualizing the dark green Buddha and reciting his mantra *oṃ amoghasiddhi āḥ hūṃ*. I shall end this chapter with a true story about an Amoghasiddhi devotee. I include it to show that, though we have talked so much in these chapters about the Buddhas as symbols, the effects they have on the lives of those who meditate upon them are very tangible.

The hero of our story was interested in climbing, though he was not very experienced. One weekend he went out with three much more experienced climbers onto a Scottish mountain. The climb went onto ice, on which our friend was very much a beginner. At a certain point in the climb he followed one of the others over a difficult overhang, dislodged something, and suddenly found himself in mid-air. He tumbled perhaps two hundred feet.

One of his companions rushed down to him, expecting the worst. If he wasn't dead he was bound to be injured and traumatized. Even tough climbers were likely to be calling for their mothers after such an experience. But our friend wasn't dead, and he wasn't crying. He was lying in the snow, with two broken ankles, laughing. His companions were amazed. It was preposterous that he should have fallen so far, nearly killed himself, and yet be so cheerful.

The reason he was laughing was that he had seen something as he fell. As he tumbled headlong, he had found himself suddenly travelling down a long, dark tunnel. At the end, waiting for him, was a dark green Buddha, his hand held in the gesture of dispelling all fear. He had meditated on Amoghasiddhi for several years, trying to see the figure clearly. Now in response, in a moment of supreme danger, Amoghasiddhi had come to his aid. The green Buddha appeared to him far more vividly than he had ever done in his meditation sessions. He was lying there laughing because he had just had the best visualization of his life.

Anyone who meditates faithfully on one of the figures described in this book can expect that at the time of their death the Buddha they have been visualizing will appear. Thus to think of these figures as merely symbols is very wrong. They can affect your everyday life. They can transcend death. In that sense they are far more 'real' than the mundane personality. If we can talk in terms of degrees of reality, then Amoghasiddhi is much more real than you or I.

Vairocana

Ten

At the Centre of the Mandala

As we saw in Chapter Five, a mandala is not a flat, two-dimensional diagram. It is more like a many-storeyed golden mansion, or even a palace of crystal, in which a light lit in one room is reflected in all the others. In the last four chapters we have entered the mandala and explored it by travelling in a circle. We could very profitably keep on circumambulating, meditating on each Buddha in turn, seeing new connections and taking the Buddhas more deeply into our consciousness. A mandala has many levels of meaning, and one cannot grasp them all at once.

However, we shall only fully understand the mandala when we have come to its centre. So how are we to arrive at the heart of the mandala? We cannot just keep walking on. It is not a case of 'go up to the northern gate, turn right, and keep walking'. We have to move in a different direction, into a 'dimensionless dimension'.

We have been well prepared to come to the heart of the mandala by the four Buddhas we have met. As we encountered them, each Buddha presented us with a gift. Each was something we needed to help prepare ourselves for a 'meeting' with ultimate Reality.

Akṣobhya held up the crystal mirror of wisdom to show us the truth of things, to let us see ourselves as we are, undistorted. Then he tapped the earth, to remind us that we shall find truth not in our ideas about things but in direct experience.

However, the clear vision of Akṣobhya could have been a little cold, a little hard. So Ratnasambhava gave us the jewel of beauty. He taught us to appreciate the beauty in nature, in the arts, in other people, in ourselves. He inspired us to mine within ourselves for the beauties of the Dharma, and to share them with others.

Then, lest we lose ourselves forever in gazing into Ratnasambhava's jewel, Amitābha gave us a red lotus. He held out to us the soft, open flower of love and compassion, so that we began to open out to others, to soften our hearts, and to see the unique value of every living thing.

Finally, with a mere gesture of his right hand, Amoghasiddhi bestowed on us the gift of fearlessness, to venture into the world energetically helping all beings. More than that, he gave us the courage to enter the centre of the mandala, to gaze upon the centre of existence.

We need the gift of fearlessness because, according to some Buddhist traditions, we have come to the centre of the mandala before, and every time it has been such an overpowering experience that we have retreated from it. The *Tibetan Book of the Dead* describes how, after physical death, consciousness goes through various stages of dissociation from the physical body. Once this process is complete, one encounters the 'clear light of the Void' – the dazzling radiance of ultimate Reality. However, this experience is usually too much for us, so we run away. From a taste of non-duality, we retreat into dualistic experience. Our consciousness reverts to its habitual interpretation of experience in terms of a subject confronted by external objects. Then, one by one, there appear to us archetypal visions of the Buddhas of the mandala. If we were to recognize them for what they are, we should free ourselves from the whole cycle of birth and death. However, they are so awe-inspiring that we are terrified and unable to recognize them as projections of our own mind. So we keep running away from Reality.

As time goes on in this intermediate state, we 'move down' through different levels of consciousness, our mental processes become increasingly polarized between subject and object, until at last we reach a level on which we feel secure. It is on that level that we take rebirth. (This is describing the process from the 'common sense' viewpoint of the ego. It might be closer to the truth to say that, having become extremely concentrated in the early part of the death process, consciousness becomes increasingly diffuse once again through the force of the mind's centrifugal tendencies to craving and aversion.)

One way in which we can change this pattern of fear and avoidance is by meditating on the mandala of the five Buddhas. If we have repeatedly visualized the Buddhas and thoroughly familiarized ourselves with them while we are alive, then when we die we shall not be dazzled and overpowered. In the bardo (Tibetan, *antarābhava* in Sanskrit)[27] after death, we shall move towards them as old friends, and will identify with them and their empty nature, and thus gain insight into Reality. It will be a useful first step if we can practise approaching the centre of the mandala in imagination.

The illuminator

> Light is, in reality, more awful than darkness. (Ruskin)

Our life has ended. One by one the signs of death have appeared. The grosser physical elements have sunk into the more subtle. We are no longer in contact with the body. For a brief period the clear light of Reality has dawned upon us. Clear, luminous, and knowing, it is the nature of the mind. If we could recognize it we should attain the *dharmakāya*, the 'truth body' of a Buddha, and gain Enlightenment. However, without considerable meditational training, it is difficult to recognize this experience for what it is. If we fail to do so we lapse into unconsciousness, out of which the sequence of visions of the Buddhas of the mandala begins.

Ahead of us is a terrible radiance. As we find ourselves drawn towards it, there is a vast white light, and a great roaring sound. Remembering the upraised hand of Amoghasiddhi we allow ourselves to move closer, to enter the radiance and the roaring.

As we accept the situation and become one with the light, everything changes. Suddenly, all is calm and stillness. It is as though we had entered the eye of a hurricane. We become accustomed to the brilliant light. The roaring ceases. We see that the roars came from four great lions, who are supporting a lotus throne on their backs. Above the lions, everything is white light: there is a white lotus, a white moon mat, and a white Buddha, smiling and serene, the colour of sunlight on snow, wearing ornate white robes. The only contrast is provided by his black hair, and a great golden wheel which he clasps in his hands with a peculiar mudrā. This is Vairocana (Tibetan *Namnang*), the Buddha whose name means 'illuminator'. In the Nyingma system of practice which we are following here, it is he who sits in the heart of the mandala, the symbol and embodiment of absolute Reality. (In some forms of Tantric practice, Vairocana is in the east, with Akṣobhya at the centre of the mandala.[28])

The golden wheel which Vairocana holds is the last gift of the Buddhas – the final thing we need. If we meditate on it long enough we shall arrive at Enlightenment.

The golden wheel and sovereignty

This golden wheel is rich in symbolic meanings. It suggests a number of qualities, all of which are attributes of Vairocana, of the experience of arriving at total Enlightenment (for it is only with Enlightenment that we can calmly take our seat at the centre of the mandala).

In the Indian Buddhist mind, the golden wheel was associated with sovereignty. It is the emblem of the wheel-turning king (*cakravartin-rāja*), a monarch who rules in accordance with the Dharma. Being a sincere Dharma practitioner himself, he uses the authority of his position to influence society in all kinds of positive ways. The descriptions of his attributes in Buddhist scriptures are important, as they serve as a reminder that Buddhism is concerned not just with individual development and retreat from the world. Buddhism aims to influence and transform society. This is worth doing in itself, but it also comes from the recognition that individual Dharma practice becomes extremely difficult if the culture and society in which you live are unsupportive of, or hostile towards, your efforts.

There have been a number of historical examples of rulers who greatly influenced their territories by propagating the Dharma. The best known is the Indian emperor Aśoka. Originally a warrior emperor in the mode of Alexander the Great, he was so sickened by the carnage involved in his conquest of the state of Kalinga that he renounced violence altogether and embraced Buddhism. From then on, he maintained peace throughout his vast territories, built monasteries, supported the Buddhist monastic sangha, and established hospitals and schools. In India one can still see remains of stone pillars inscribed with Aśoka's addresses to his subjects. In them he explains the reasons for his conversion to Buddhism, urges his subjects to practise it, and makes decrees to regulate various aspects of life in accordance with the Dharma.[29]

Another good example of a monarch who enabled the Dharma profoundly to influence his country is the Tibetan king Trisong Detsen. He invited Buddhist teachers to come from India to introduce the Dharma to Tibet. In particular, he encouraged the great Tantric guru Padmasambhava to spend time there. In collaboration they created the great monastery of Samye.

The association of the wheel with kingship comes partly from an ancient Indian tradition, according to which the boundaries of a kingdom were established by setting loose a horse with a wheel on its back. Wherever it went unchallenged, the king's rule was accepted.

Another word for the Buddha's teaching is *sāsana*. This means something like dispensation – the area over which an Enlightened mind holds sway. As the principles of the Dharma hold true throughout all universes, and there is nothing in time or space that can shake the mind of a Buddha, which encompasses it all, then in a sense the whole of time and space is the Buddha's domain, the sphere of influence of the Enlightened mind, of Vairocana.

In Buddhist history there are many episodes which set the attributes of a king or emperor (the highest of men in power and rank) against a Buddha or other Enlightened teacher, who has reached the pinnacle of human perfection. One thinks of Bodhidharma's meeting with the Chinese emperor, Padmasambhava's with Trisong Detsen, or the monk Nāgasena's debates with King Milinda. In every case it is the sovereign who is forced to bow down and acknowledge that the guru is beyond his power.[30]

One finds repeated instances of this in the life of the Buddha Śākyamuni. We have seen how at the time of his birth Asita prophesied that Siddhārtha would become either a great ruler or a Buddha. Despite his father's best efforts, he came to see that ultimately even the greatest ruler has no control over anything; like Canute he is unable to hold back the waves of change, of sickness, and of death. A Buddha, on the other hand, in becoming master of his own consciousness, becomes possessed of the universe.

When, after his Enlightenment, the Buddha visited his family, his father reproached him for not wearing the robes befitting one of noble birth. The Buddha retorted that he came from the noblest lineage of all, that of the Enlightened, and that the rag robes he wore were the traditional garb of that noble lineage.

These paradoxes are made much of in the sūtras. Though the Buddha is a beggar, he is more noble than the greatest king. Though he has nothing, his life is more pleasurable. Though he is unarmed, a king surrounded by his army is more frightened than he.

To give one small example, there is a story in the *Udāna*[31] – a collection of suttas in the Pali canon – of a monk called Bhaddiya, who used to be a king. His friends hear him sitting in the forest saying 'Ah, 'tis bliss, 'tis bliss!' They assume that he is recalling his days of pleasure and comfort as a king, and is dissatisfied with the spiritual life. They tell the Buddha this. He refuses to jump to conclusions, but asks Bhaddiya to come and see him, and questions him. Bhaddiya recounts how when he was a king he had a palace guarded inside and out, and still he felt his life was at risk. By comparison, the simple life of mental training in the forest is sheer bliss.

These stories counteract the idea some people have that followers of the spiritual life are too weak and inadequate to succeed in the world. On the contrary, the Buddhist tradition shows that spiritual practitioners become kings among men and queens among women – there are similar stories of female practitioners, and various queens have practised the Dharma. There is an important Mahāyāna sūtra called *The Lion's Roar of Queen Srimala*.[32]

The spiritual life surpasses even the most elevated of worldly states, and it requires at least as much energy and courage to extend the empire of the Dharma as it does to extend a worldly kingdom. Not for nothing did the Buddha say that someone who had gained a spiritual victory over his lower nature had gained a greater victory than that involved in conquering a thousand men a thousand times in battle.

So the first message of the golden wheel is that by setting out on the spiritual path one joins the most noble of all lineages. Without preening ourselves or inflating our egos, if we are practitioners of the Dharma we should recognize that we need envy no one. The golden wheel also reminds us that we are practising so as to be able one day to affect all people. It helps us see that we cannot forget the world and society, but have to work positively within it, to create positive conditions for ourselves and others to practise the Dharma.

The golden wheel as solar symbol

Vairocana means 'illuminator', and it is clear that the golden wheel he holds in his hands is, symbolically, a great sun. The sun, of course, has legions of associations attached to it. In some cultures the sun is seen as a golden door to a higher dimension. In fact, just as all natural life depends upon it, the sun as symbol plays a major role in the 'psychic economy' of all human beings. For the visionary or mystic it becomes far more than a ball of gas, and represents the spiritual principle that illumines the universe.

There are two attributes of the sun which make it a particularly appropriate symbol for Buddhahood. The first is the sun's centrality. It is the heart of the planets' dance. Drawn to its light and warmth, even cold Neptune and Pluto follow it like lovers. You could look at the mandala as a kind of planetary system, with four planets – blue, yellow, red, and green – in orbit around Vairocana's golden wheel, and all deriving their light from it. For, in a sense, the other four Buddhas are just partial reflections of Vairocana.

His family is known simply as the Buddha or Tathāgata family (*Tathāgata*, meaning 'thus gone', is another epithet for someone who is fully Enlightened.) His Wisdom, the *Dharmadhātu* (sphere of truth) Wisdom, is the totality of all wisdom, embracing all those of the other Buddhas. His white colour includes all colours, and the other hues of the mandala are fragmentations of his pure whiteness. It is his energy and intensity, his purity, which we are seeing in other parts of the mandala, just as we see the sun through the brilliant pieces of a great stained-glass window.

The second attribute, complementing the first, is the sun's all-pervasiveness. The sun itself is like the hub of the golden wheel, the spokes its rays, and the rim the boundary of its vast sphere of influence. As the wheel is a perfect circle, it suggests the absolute even-mindedness of the Enlightened Mind, its compassion shining equally on everything and everyone.

The golden wheel symbolizes the paradoxical nature of Vairocana. He sits at the centre of the mandala, at its hub, yet the experience of total Enlightenment that he symbolizes is one of panoramic awareness without any central reference point. Vairocana is central to the whole mandala only in the sense that his Dharmadhātu Wisdom is the central experience of the spiritual life. In achieving this Wisdom we feel perfectly balanced, completely in harmony with everything. Yet, on attaining that Dharmadhātu Wisdom, we find that notions of centre and circumference disappear. There is no 'I' at the centre of the mandala to which everything is referred. At the centre of the mandala we find only panoramic awareness which embraces the whole mandala. It is for this reason that Vairocana's Pure Land is called the All-Pervading Circle, and his element is space.

The golden wheel as symbol of the Dharma

The Buddha's first teaching, to his old comrades in asceticism, is traditionally referred to as his first 'turning, or setting in motion, of the wheel of the Dharma' (Sanskrit *dharmacakrapravartana*). The mudrā with which Vairocana holds the wheel is known as the mudrā of turning the wheel of the Dharma. The golden wheel, then, symbolizes not only Buddhahood itself but also the Buddha's teaching, which leads to that Enlightened state. It is usually shown with eight spokes, which symbolize the Noble Eightfold Path. It is one of the commonest of all Buddhist symbols. The great Buddhist monastic university of Nālandā had as its crest this *dharmacakra*, supported on each side by deer – a reminder of the Deer Park at Sarnath where the Buddha first taught.

It seems likely that the figure of Vairocana appeared out of meditation on the Buddha Śākyamuni as teacher, which from our point of view is his most crucial function: if he had not bothered to teach there would be no Buddhism, and the path to Enlightenment would not be open to us. In the Mahāyāna sūtras Śākyamuni is represented continuing to teach, eternally turning the wheel of the Dharma, seated on the Vulture's Peak. In the Mahāyāna sūtras it is transformed into the archetypal seat of teaching of the Buddha. Vairocana symbolizes this eternal teaching of the Dharma. He reminds us that within our own mind there always exists the possibility of total transformation.

In a sense, we are confronting Vairocana's radiance all the time, although it is dimmed and diffused. However, this very phrase gives the game away. As long as 'we' are confronting 'it', we cannot be at the centre of the mandala. Our difficulty is that there is an 'I' which stands apart from Reality, and experiences it as something outside ourselves. We remain cut off from it because we do not identify with all our experience. Very often, our identification is entirely with our physical body, and its limited concerns. The rest of life we see as being separate from us. This, according to Buddhism, is the dark well-spring of all suffering.

How can we overcome this situation, where we are confronted by Reality but feel cut off from it? There are two strategies we can try in order to ease the tension we feel. The first is what we might call 'ego-imperialism'. We can set out to conquer the world as object, to subdue it, and bring it under our sway. We can try to control what happens in it. We can make sexual conquests; we can compete – fighting our way to the top of the pile. This strategy can never work. Apart from anything else, with so many million other egos all battling to do the same thing, there are astronomical odds against our succeeding.

What is the alternative? The other option requires a complete change of perspective. It involves giving up all attempts at power and control, and relating to the world through loving-kindness. It is this turnabout in our attitude that is required by the first precept taken by all Buddhists. It is usually expressed in negative terms, as undertaking not to harm living beings. However, if we plumb its significance to the depths, we see that there is far more involved than not blacking eyes or swatting flies. It involves giving up the central place we give to our egotistical interests and concerns, not using even the subtlest force or manipulation to obtain what we want but relating to the world and other people with a cooperative spirit, from a basis of loving-kindness.

This is a very major change indeed. In trying to make it we may feel something of the resistance that men of the sixteenth century felt towards the Copernican theory that their world was not at the centre of the universe, but was just another participant in the planets' dance around the sun. If we do manage to give up 'ego-imperialism', then our attention is no longer narrowed down, fixated on our own concerns. Through loving-kindness we expand our consciousness to include more and more people. Then our minds begin to take on more of the expansive and all-pervading quality of Vairocana's Wisdom. We come closer to Reality, closer to the centre of the mandala.

Through loving-kindness, we subdue the lions of our acquisitive territorial nature and harness their energies to support the throne of our spiritual life. We open our hearts to other people like an unfolding white lotus. As the process continues, our receptivity is not towards other people seen just as separate egos. We experience the Reality which shines through all people, all experience, until at last we lay down our limited self as a moon mat at the feet of Enlightenment, to reflect its golden sunlight. Thus we create the lotus throne on which a radiant white Buddha can take his seat. The consciousness of this Buddha is panoramic, not limited to any fixed reference point in time or space, illuminating the whole universe. As such he is sovereign over all the worlds, and holds the golden wheel of spiritual kingship.

When we have seen through egotism and embraced loving-kindness towards all that lives, we shall be ready to receive Vairocana's gift, the golden wheel – the final thing we need to complete our development, the last lesson we have to learn from our meditation on the mandala. What shall we do with this gift? If we accept the *dharmacakra* there is only one thing we can do with it, and that is to turn it, to set it in motion. In other words we have to teach. Of course, this does not necessarily mean that we have to teach Buddhism in any formal sense. 'Teaching' here means passing on what we have gained from our exploration of the mandala. The gift Vairocana gives us is the responsibility of sharing what we have learned with others. The final message of the mandala is that no experience is complete until it has been communicated. We can say that it would not have been enough for Śākyamuni to spend the rest of his life sitting under the bodhi tree rapt with the bliss of Enlightenment. In a sense, his experience of Enlightenment was only complete and fulfilling when he saw it mirrored in the understanding eyes of Kauṇḍinya.

If we practise Buddhism, or study the Dharma, and then do not pass on what we have gained, we have not heard the message of Vairocana. Keeping the Dharma to oneself is a kind of ego imperialism. In a Pali sutta the Buddha tells his disciples that he has held nothing back from them in 'the closed fist of the teacher'.[33] In the *Saddharma Puṇḍarīka Sūtra* ('Lotus of the Wonderful Law') the Buddha is said to offer the Dharma to the world unstintingly, like a great rain-cloud pouring water upon the thirsty earth.

Once we have entered and explored the mandala, it will not be enough to use its blueprint to make our own life a harmonious pattern. That is only the beginning. We have to enable all suffering sentient beings, all life, to come to the centre of the mandala. This is the task of the Bodhisattva, on whom we shall focus in the next book in this series.

Before then, we can look at one last association of the golden wheel, which indicates how the mandala keeps expanding, how it is never finished, how it has within it the seeds of its own self-transcendence.

We have seen that the golden wheel is the sun of Reality, toward which we need to orientate our lives. It is a symbol of the Buddha's spiritual kingship over the universe. It is also a symbol for the teaching, and the need to complete our experience of the spiritual path by sharing it with others. However, there is a further possible interpretation, which adds another dimension of meaning. This golden wheel that Vairocana holds could also be seen as the golden circle of the mandala itself.

Vairocana sits at the centre of the mandala, but paradoxically he is at the same time completely beyond it, holding it lightly in his hands, spinning it like a child's toy. Every step on the spiritual path, every step around the mandala, is an experience of self-transcendence. This is true not just of the path. Even the goal, Buddhahood itself, is a continuing process of evolution – moving to higher and higher levels in ways we cannot conceive. That is why, at the centre of the mandala, we meet a Buddha holding the mandala. At the centre of the mandala we transcend mandalas altogether.

CORRELATIONS	AKṢOBHYA	RATNASAMBHAVA
Meaning of Name	The Immutable or Imperturbable	The Jewel-Born or Jewel-Producing
Colour	Deep blue	Yellow
Direction	East	South
Time of day	Dawn	Noon
Emblem	Vajra	Jewel
Family or kula	Vajra	Ratna
Family Protector	Vajrapāṇi	Ratnapāṇi
Animal	Elephant	Horse
Mudra	Earth-touching (bhūmisparśa)	Supreme Giving (vārada)
Seed syllable	hūṃ	trāṃ
Mantra	oṃ vajra akṣobhya hūṃ	oṃ ratnasambhava trāṃ
Wisdom	Mirror-Like	Sameness
Poison	Hatred	Pride
Skandha	Form	Feeling
Element	Water	Earth
Vijñāna	Relative ālaya	Manas, or defiled mental consciousness
Pure Land	Abhirati (the Joyous)	Śrīmat (The Glorious)
Consort	Locana	Māmakī
Reflex	Vajrasattva	—
Wrathful form	Vajra Heruka	Ratna Heruka
Attendant Bodhisattvas	Kṣitigarbha, Maitreya	Ākāśagarbha, Samantabhadra
Attendant goddesses	Lāsyā, Puṣpa	Mālā, Dhūpa
Protector of gate	Vijaya	Yamāntaka
Vidyadhara	Established in the Stages	Lord of Life
Other family members	Most wrathful yidams	Jambhala, Vasundharā, The windhorse
Day in bardo	Second	Third
Associated chakra	Heart	Navel
Realm	Hells	Human
Magical function	Destroying	Increasing, enriching, Harvest magic

AMITĀBHA	AMOGHASIDDHI	VAIROCANA
Infinite Light	Unobstructed Success	The Illuminator
Red	Green	White
West	North	Centre
Sunset	Midnight	—
Lotus	Double vajra or sword	Golden *dharmacakra*
Padma	Karma	Buddha or Tathāgata
Avalokiteśvara	Viṣvapāṇi	Mañjuśrī
Peacock	*Garuḍa* or bird-man	Lion
Meditation (*dhyāna*)	Fearlessness (*abhaya*)	Turning the Wheel of the Dharma
hrīḥ	*āḥ*	*oṃ*
oṃ amideva hrīḥ	*oṃ amoghasiddhi āḥ hūṃ*	*oṃ vairocana hūṃ*
Discriminating	All-Accomplishing	Dharmadhātu
Greed	Envy	Ignorance
Saṃjñā (recognition or apperception)	Volition	Consciousness
Fire	Air	Space
Manovijñāna, or consciousness of mental objects	Five sense consciousnesses	Absolute *ālaya*
Sukhāvatī (the Happy Land)	Karmasampat (Perfected Good Actions)	Ghanavyūha (All-Pervading Circle)
Pāṇḍaravāsinī	Samaya Tārā	Ākāśadhāteśvarī
Amitāyus	—	—
Padma Heruka	Karma Heruka	Buddha Heruka
Avalokiteśvara, Mañjuśrī	Vajrapāṇi, Sarvanīvaraṇaviṣkambhin	—
Gīta, Aloka	Gandha, Naivedya	—
Hayagrīva	Amṛtakuṇḍalin	—
Great Symbol	Spontaneously Arisen	Lotus Lord of Dance
Śākyamuni, Kurukullā, Tārā, Padmasambhava, Padmanarteśvara	—	—
Fourth	Fifth	First
Throat	Base	Crown
Hungry ghosts (*pretas*)	*Asuras* or titans	Gods
Attraction, fascination	Pacifying, or all functions	Pacifying

Notes

1   It is sometimes said that both teachers asked Siddhārtha to co-lead their groups, but this is based on a mistranslation of a passage in the *Majjhima Nikāya*.

2   Kauṇḍinya in Pali is Koṇḍañña.

3   See Bhadantachariya Buddhaghosa, *The Path of Purification*, trans. Bhikkhu Ñāṇamoli, Buddhist Publication Society, 1975, pp.126–84.

4   Nyanatiloka, *Buddhist Dictionary*, 4th edition, Buddhist Publication Society, 1980, p.20.

5   Though I speak of the early Buddhists concentrating on the Buddha's *nirmāṇakāya*, this is itself a late term, not one that they themselves would have used.

6   These are traditionally known as the four *saṃgrahavastus*. For more information see Sangharakshita, *The Inconceivable Emancipation*, Windhorse Publications, 1995, pp.51–4.

7   The ending of the famous 'Song of Meditation' (*Zazen Wasan*) – by the Zen master Hakuin Ekaku (1685–1768), based on the translation in *A First Zen Reader*, compiled and trans. Trevor Leggett, Charles E. Tuttle, 1960.

8   Other systems of the five Buddhas relate to Tantric texts such as the *Tattvasaṃgraha* or *Symposium of Truth*, and the *Guhyasamāja*. For details see David L. Snellgrove, *Indo-Tibetan Buddhism*, Serindia, 1987. The *Bardo Thödol* gives the Nyingma understanding of the after-death process; for the views of another school see *Death, Intermediate State and Rebirth* in Selected Reading.

9   Dr Jeffrey Hopkins lists many of these meanings in his introduction to *Kalachakra Tantra: Rite of Initiation*, Wisdom Publications, 1988.

10 This is the definition given by Rongzompa Chokyi Zangpo, translated for me by John Peacock.

11 Here I am emphatically not equating Enlightenment with the psychic integration achieved through the Jungian individuation process, though clearly psychological integration is a sound basis for higher spiritual attainments.

12 From W.B. Yeats, 'The Second Coming'.

13 The different features of the mandala can be interpreted in various ways. For example, the spiritual path is sometimes divided into the three stages of renunciation, Bodhicitta (the compassionate desire to help all living beings to be free from suffering) and wisdom. (See for instance Tsongkhapa's short text 'The Three Principles of the Path' in Geshe Wangyal's *The Door of Liberation*, Wisdom Publications, 1995, pp.135–7.) According to one explanation, these three stages are represented by the rings of cremation grounds, vajras, and flames of the mandala. See Geshe Kelsang Gyatso, *A Guide To Dakiniland*, Tharpa, 1991, pp.119–20.

14 Some Yogācāra texts enumerate only seven consciousnesses.

15 They are also sometimes called the '*dhyāni* Buddhas', a term which is not traditional but was coined by an English writer in the nineteenth century.

16 This view of 'seeds' being put into a 'store' and remaining inactive until they ripen is useful up to a point, but it is a very static model of a dynamic process. The Buddhist Dzogchen system, preserved and practised mainly within the Nyingma school of Tibetan Buddhism, has a far more dynamic view of the process. It thinks not of seeds but of 'habitual propensities' (Tibetan *bakchak*), which are in a constant process of being stirred within a 'stratum' or 'matrix' of consciousness (Tibetan *kunzhi nampar shepa*), which in itself is inactive. This *kunzhi nampar shepa* is the basis of both saṃsāra and nirvāṇa.

17 For example, in the *Mahāsaccaka Sutta*, the 36th sutta of the *Majjhima Nikāya* (MN i.247–8).

18 In Greek myth, Procrustes was a robber who fitted travellers into his bed by stretching or lopping their limbs until they were the right size for it.

19 *Entering the Path of Enlightenment*, trans. Marion L. Matics, George Allen and Unwin, 1970, p.154.

20 Ibid., p.155.

21 This is the eighteenth vow in the Chinese translation of Sanghavarman. It is missing in the Sanskrit. See the note by the Reverend Bunyiu Nanjio in *Buddhist Mahāyāna Texts*, Dover Publications, 1969, p.73.

22 See Glossary for an explanation of the term *reflex*.

23 This story is told in Trevor Leggett's excellent collection of translations of Japanese Zen texts *A Second Zen Reader*, Charles E. Tuttle, 1988.

24 Lama Anagarika Govinda, *Foundations of Tibetan Mysticism*, Weiser Books, 1969, p.262.

25 See for example Aśvaghoṣa's *Buddhacharita*, in *Buddhist Mahāyāna Texts*, Dover Publications, 1969, pp.164–5. A Pali source of the same story is the *Udāna*, chapter 2.

26 According to Alice Getty (*The Gods of Northern Buddhism*, Charles E. Tuttle, 1962, p.42), Amoghasiddhi is represented in Nepalese stupas with a canopy of snakes over his head. She also describes a *thangka* of the five Buddhas in the British Museum in which the fifth has a snake coiled beside him.

27 The Tibetan word *bardo* just means between – i.e. the state of consciousness between any two other states of consciousness. For example, sleep is a bardo between two periods of waking consciousness. However, the term is used especially for the period between death and rebirth.

28 It is in the Highest Tantra of the New Translation schools (such as the Sakya, Kagyu, and Geluk) that Akṣobhya becomes the central figure. See F.D. Lessing and A. Wayman, *Introduction to the Buddhist Tantric Systems*, Motilal Banarsidass, 1978, pp.101–3.

29 It has to be said that in his edicts Aśoka uses the word *dharma* very unclearly, and talks quite often about 'going to heaven'. Some scholars believe Aśoka was exploiting an ambiguity by which the term *dharma* is used both within the Hindu brahminical tradition and with Buddhist meanings.

30 For an account of Bodhidharma's meeting with Emperor Wu of Liang, see the first case in the *koan* collection called *The Blue Cliff Record*, trans. Cleary and Cleary, Shambhala, 1977, vol.1. Padmasambhava's meeting with the King of Tibet occurs in Canto 61, 'The Refusal to Make Obeisance upon Meeting with the King of Tibet' in *The Life and Liberation of Padmasambhava*, Dharma Publishing, 1978. The debates of the Greek king Menander with the monk Nāgasena are recorded in *The Questions of King Milinda* (2 vols), trans. T.W. Rhys Davids, Dover Publications, 1963.

31 *Udāna* ii.10.

32 *The Lion's Roar of Queen Srimala*, trans. Alex Wayman and Hideko Wayman, Columbia University Press, 1974.

33 In the *Mahāparinibbāna Sutta*, the 16th sutta of the *Dīgha Nikāya* (DN ii.100).

Illustration Credits

Colour plates

PLATE ONE Śākyamuni thangka by permission of the London Buddhist Centre.

PLATE TWO Vajrasattva thangka by permission of the Rupa Company, Kathmandu.

PLATE THREE Amitāyus thangka by permission of Urgyen Sangharakshita.

PLATES FOUR TO EIGHT Details from five Jina mandala by permission of Dhammachari Amoghavamsa.

PLATE NINE Thousand-armed Avalokiteśvara thangka by permission of the London
Buddhist Centre.

PLATE TEN Four-armed Avalokiteśvara thangka by permission of Clear Vision.

PLATE ELEVEN Mañjuśrī thangka by permission of ITBCI School, Kalimpong. Photographed by Dhammarati.

Black and White Illustrations

PAGE 20 Detail of Śākyamuni thangka by permission of Dhammachari Maitreya.

PAGE 58 Detail of five Jinas from Vajrasattva thangka. See Plate Two.

PAGE 63 Amitābha thangka by permission of Dhammachari Dharmaghosha.

PAGE 70 Akṣobhya drawing by Dhammachari Chintamani.

PAGE 73 Vajra drawing by Dhammachari Aloka.

Glossary

ĀLAYA VIJÑĀNA   Literally 'store consciousness'. According to the system of the Yogācāra (q.v.), the *ālaya* is the most fundamental level of the mind. It has two aspects. The relative *ālaya* acts as a repository of the imprints of all one's volitions. The absolute *ālaya* is unconditioned and beyond all suffering. To experience it is to become aware of the true nature of things.

ANIMAL REALM   The realm of existence in which consciousness is dominated by the struggle for survival and the basic drives for food, sex, and sleep. It may refer to actual animals or to human beings in such states of consciousness.

ARCHETYPAL REALM   The objective pole of a supernormal level of consciousness. A level of heightened experience on which everything is imbued with rich symbolic meaning.

ARCHETYPE   A deep patterning of the mind, which often expresses itself through myth and symbol. Archetypal experience is often tinged with a feeling of supra-personal reality.

ASURA   Similar to the Titans of Greek mythology, asuras are powerful and jealous beings who are prepared to use force and manipulation to gain their own ends. In the Wheel of Life (q.v.) they are represented as warring with the gods. They may be seen as objectively-existent beings or as symbols for states of mind sometimes experienced by human beings. Female asuras are called asurīs and are represented as voluptuous. Asurīs play on their seductive charms to gain their own ends.

BARDO   (*Tibetan*) The 'state between' two other states of being. In particular the intermediate state between one life and the next.

BHIKSHU   A Buddhist monk.

BODHICITTA   The compassionate 'desire' (based not on egoistic volitions but insight into the true nature of things) to gain Enlightenment for the benefit of all living beings. More technically, it can be divided into absolute Bodhicitta, which is synonymous with transcendental wisdom, and relative Bodhicitta – the heartfelt compassion that is the natural consequence of an experience of absolute Bodhicitta.

BODHISATTVA   A being pledged to become a Buddha so as to be in the best position to help all other beings to escape from suffering by gaining Enlightenment.

BRAHMA VIHĀRAS, FOUR   loving-kindness (*maitrī*), compassion (*karuṇā*), sympathetic joy (*muditā*), and equanimity (*upekṣā*).

BUDDHA   A title, meaning one who is awake. A Buddha is someone who has gained Enlightenment – the perfection of wisdom and compassion. In particular, the title applied to Siddhārtha Gautama, also known as Śākyamuni, the founder of Buddhism.

BUDDHA FAMILY   The five main groupings into which every aspect of existence – both mundane and transcendental – is divided in Tantric Buddhism. The blueprint for these groupings is provided by the mandala of the five Jinas (q.v.).

BUDDHAS, FIVE   Another name for the five Jinas (q.v.).

CHAKRA   Literally 'wheel'. (Anglicized, from the Sanskrit *cakra*.) Centres of energy visualized within the body in some forms of Buddhist Tantric meditation.

CITTAMĀTRA   Literally 'Mind Only'. A school of Mahāyāna Buddhism, initiated by the fourth-century Indian teacher Asaṅga, which denies that there is any ultimate distinction between mind and matter. Also known as the Yogācāra school.

CLEAR LIGHT   The experience of the natural state of the mind, of consciousness 'undiluted' by any tendency to move towards sensory experience. Recognition of the nature of this state is synonymous with Enlightenment.

COMPLETION STAGE   The second of the two stages of Highest Tantra (q.v.). It focuses on advanced practices designed to concentrate and channel the most subtle energies of the psychophysical organism, in order to bring about the speedy attainment of Enlightenment.

CONDITIONED EXISTENCE   See saṃsāra.

ḌĀKINĪ   A class of beings who appear in the form of women (though they may sometimes be represented with the heads of animals). They may be more or less evolved, from fiends and witches to Enlightened beings. In the Buddhist Tantra they often function as messengers, and frequently represent upsurging inspiration or non-conceptual understanding.

DEVA   A long-lived being who experiences refined and blissful states of mind. Devas thus inhabit a heavenly realm. These realms can be interpreted as objective or as symbols for states of mind in which human beings can dwell.

DHARMA   A word with numerous meanings. Among other things it can mean truth or reality. It also stands for all those teachings and methods which are conducive to gaining Enlightenment, and thereby seeing things as they truly are, particularly the teachings of the Buddha.

DHARMACAKRA   The 'Wheel of the Truth'. A large golden wheel, symbolic of the Buddha's teaching.

DHARMAKĀYA   Literally 'body of truth'. The mind of a Buddha. The Enlightened experience, unmediated by concepts or symbols.

DHARMAPĀLA   A protector of the Dharma. Buddhism recognizes many Dharmapālas. Some may be expressions of the Enlightened mind, others are beings on a mundane level who are sympathetic to the Dharma.

DHYĀNA   A state of supernormal concentration on a wholesome object. It may occur spontaneously, but is generally the fruit of successful meditation practice. Buddhist tradition recognizes different levels of dhyāna, each one increasingly refined and satisfying.

EIGHTFOLD PATH   The path leading to the extinction of all suffering and unsatisfactoriness, consisting of right, or perfect, vision, emotion, speech, action, livelihood, effort, mindfulness, and meditation.

EMPTINESS   See śūnyatā.

ENLIGHTENMENT   A state of perfect wisdom and limitless compassion. The only permanently satisfying solution to the human predicament. The achievement of a Buddha.

ESOTERIC REFUGES   Those Refuges (q.v.) which are matters of direct personal experience, embodied in the guru, yidam, and ḍākinī (all q.v.) by the Buddhist Tantra.

GARUḌA   A species of mythical bird, enemy of the nāgas (q.v.).

GENERATION STAGE   The first of the two stages of Highest Tantra (q.v.). It focuses on the development of the vivid visualization and experience of oneself as a deity.

GESHE (*Tibetan*) A title awarded in the Kadam and Geluk schools of Tibetan Buddhism to those who have become deeply accomplished in Buddhist studies. The word *geshe* relates to the Sanskrit *kalyāṇa mitra*, meaning spiritual friend – so a *geshe* in the true sense is one who can act as a wise and learned spiritual advisor.

GOING FOR REFUGE   The act of committing oneself to the attainment of Enlightenment by reliance on the three Refuges (q.v.). Also refers to the ceremony by which one formally becomes a Buddhist.

GURU   A person who through teaching and/or personal example helps other people to follow the path to Enlightenment.

HIGHEST TANTRA   The most advanced of the four levels of Buddhist Tantra. It consists of the Generation and Completion stages (both q.v.).

HĪNAYĀNA   The 'lesser way' or 'lesser vehicle'. Buddhist schools who do not advocate the Bodhisattva ideal. Though in common use among Mahāyāna and Vajrayāna Buddhists, the term is regarded as pejorative by the Theravāda school (q.v.).

HUMAN REALM   The state of being 'truly human' – characterized by a balanced awareness of both the pleasant and painful aspects of life, and a capacity to cooperate and empathize with other human beings. In Buddhism this state is regarded as the best starting-point from which to enter the path to Enlightenment.

HUNGRY GHOST   A class of being (*preta* in Sanskrit) too overcome by craving to gain satisfaction from any experience. The idea can be interpreted literally, or symbolically as a state of mind sometimes experienced by human beings. Pretas are represented in Buddhist art with large stomachs and pinhole mouths.

JEWELS, THREE   The Buddha, Dharma, and Sangha (all q.v.). The three highest values in Buddhism.

JINAS, FIVE   A very important set of five Buddhas, often represented as interrelated in a mandala (q.v.) pattern. They each embody a particular Wisdom (Sanskrit *jñāna*) – an aspect of the Enlightened vision. Jina literally means 'conqueror'.

KARMA   Literally 'action'. Simply stated, the so-called 'law of karma' says that our willed actions (mental and vocal as well as physical) will have consequences for us in the future. 'Skilful' actions arising from states of love, tranquillity, and wisdom, will result in happiness. 'Unskilful' actions, based on craving, aversion, and ignorance, will produce painful results.

KĀYA   Literally 'body'. A Buddha is said to have a number of *kāyas*. They represent Enlightenment on different levels of experience, or as experienced by beings on different levels of consciousness.

KULA   Literally 'family'. Can refer to a group of Tantric practitioners, or to the Buddha families (q.v.).

LAMA   (*Tibetan*) see guru.

MAHĀYĀNA   The 'great way' or 'great vehicle'. Those schools of Buddhism that teach the Bodhisattva ideal – of selfless striving to gain Enlightenment so as to be in the best possible position to help all other living beings to escape from suffering.

MAITRĪ   Universal friendliness or universal loving-kindness. One of the four *brahma vihāras* (q.v).

MANDALA   A word with various meanings in different contexts. In this book it means a pattern of elements around a central focus. Ideal mandalas are often used as objects of meditation in Buddhist Tantra.

MANTRA   A string of sound-symbols recited to concentrate and protect the mind. Many Buddhist figures have mantras associated with them. Through reciting their mantra one deepens one's connection with the aspect of Enlightenment which the figure embodies.

MĀRA   The Buddhist personification of everything that tends to promote suffering and hinder growth towards Enlightenment. It literally means death.

MERITS   The positive states generated through the performance of virtuous actions, which predispose one to encounter happy and fortunate circumstances.

MUDRĀ   The general term for a Tantric emblem. In this book, the word is used in its sense of a hand gesture imbued with symbolic significance. In Tantric Buddhism it can also refer to a female consort.

NĀGA   A class of powerful serpents associated with water. They have something of the same associations as dragons in the West, being guardians of treasures, and associated with wisdom.

NIRMĀNAKĀYA   The physical body of a Buddha.

NIRVĀNA   The state of Enlightenment, the cessation of suffering. For the Mahāyāna (q.v.) it became a lesser ideal – a state of blissful happiness in which one could settle down rather than working compassionately to help all other beings to attain the same happy state.

NYINGMA   The oldest of the four main schools of Tibetan Buddhism, deriving its original inspiration from the Indian teacher Padmasambhava, who went to Tibet in the eighth century.

PALI CANON   The collection of teachings of Buddha Śākyamuni and some of his close disciples, originally written down in Pali, and regarded as authoritative by the Theravāda school (q.v.).

PERFECTION   (Sanskrit *pāramitā*) The main positive qualities that the Bodhisattva (q.v.) strives to develop. A positive quality only becomes a *pāramitā* in the full sense when it is imbued with transcendental wisdom. The six perfections constitute the most important list of positive qualities in Mahāyāna (q.v.) Buddhism: generosity, ethics, patience, effort, meditation, and wisdom.

PRECEPT   One of the ethical trainings recommended by the Buddha and other Buddhist teachers. There are various lists of precepts, but the most fundamental is a set of five Buddhist ethical trainings. Put in negative terms they involve working to refrain from (1) harming living beings, (2) taking the not-given, (3) sexual misconduct, (4) untruthfulness, and (5) dulling the mind with intoxicants. In positive terms this means striving to develop (1) loving-kindness, (2) generosity, (3) contentment, (4) truthfulness, and (5) awareness.

PURE LAND   A realm created through the meditative concentration and meritorious actions of a Buddha, in which beings can be reborn. In a Pure Land, conditions are totally favourable for progress towards Buddhahood. Also, the schools of Buddhism whose practice centres on being reborn in such realms.

REALMS, SIX   A classification of all the possibilities for rebirth within conditioned existence. They are the realms of the devas, asuras, humans, animals, hungry ghosts, and beings in hell (all q.v.). The six realms are pictorially represented in the Wheel of Life (q.v.).

REFLEX   Certain of the five Jinas can appear in a second form, which demonstrates another aspect of their Wisdom. This second form is sometimes described as the 'reflex' of the Jina.

REFUGE   One of the things on which Buddhism believes it is wise to rely. The three Refuges – the Buddha, the Dharma, and the Sangha – are common to all forms of Buddhism. The Esoteric Refuges (q.v.) are peculiar to Buddhist Tantra.

RIMPOCHE (OR RINPOCHE)   (*Tibetan*) An honorific title for a Tibetan Buddhist master – especially one who is believed to be the rebirth or emanation of a previous highly-developed Buddhist practitioner. It literally means 'precious one'.

SĀDHANA A general Sanskrit word for one's personal religious practice. More specifically, a Buddhist Tantric practice usually involving visualization and mantra recitation. The written text of such a Tantric practice.

ŚĀKYAMUNI The 'sage of the Śākyans', an epithet of Siddhārtha Gautama, the founder of Buddhism.

ŚĀKYANS Members of the small republic in what is now southern Nepal in which the historical Buddha was born some 2,500 years ago.

SAMAYA The commitments one takes upon oneself on receiving Vajrayāna (q.v.) initiation.

SAMBHOGAKĀYA Literally 'body of mutual enjoyment'. The radiant and glorious way in which Enlightened beings are experienced by those in supermundane states of consciousness. Can also refer to that aspect of the Enlightened experience which is concerned with speech and communication.

SAMSĀRA The cyclic round of birth and death, marked by suffering and frustration, which can only be ended by the attainment of Enlightenment.

SANGHA In the widest sense, the community of all those who are following the path to Buddhahood. As one of the Refuges (q.v.) it refers to the Ārya or Noble Sangha – those Buddhist practitioners who have gained insight into the true nature of things and whose progress towards Buddhahood is certain. In other contexts the term can refer to those who have taken ordination as Buddhist monks or nuns.

SKILFUL MEANS See upāya.

SPIRITUAL In this book, spiritual means concerned with the development of higher states of consciousness, especially with the path to Enlightenment. In this context it has nothing to do with spirits or spiritualism.

ŚŪNYATĀ Literally 'emptiness' or 'voidness'. The ultimate nature of existence, the absolute aspect of all cognizable things. The doctrine of śūnyatā holds that all phenomena are empty (*śūnya*) of any permanent unchanging self or essence. By extension, it can mean the transcendental (q.v.) experience brought about by direct intuitive insight into the empty nature of things.

SŪTRA Literally 'thread'. A discourse given by the Buddha, or by one of his senior disciples and approved by him, and included in the Buddhist canon. *Sūtra* is Sanskrit; the Pali is *sutta*.

TANTRA A form of Buddhism making use of yogic practices of visualization, mantra, mudrā, and mandalas (all q.v.), as well as symbolic ritual, and meditations which work with subtle psychophysical energies. Also the Buddhist texts, often couched in symbolic language, in which these practices are described.

TATHĀGATA   A title of the Buddha. Can mean 'one thus gone' or 'one thus come'. A Buddha goes from the world through wisdom – seeing its illusory nature. He comes into it through compassion – in order to teach living beings how to put an end to suffering.

THANGKA   (*Tibetan*) A Tibetan religious painting.

THERAVĀDA   The 'School of the Elders' – the form of Buddhism prevalent in Thailand, Burma, and Sri Lanka.

TITAN   See asura.

TRANSCENDENTAL   (Sanskrit *lokottara*). Experience that goes beyond the cyclic, mundane round of birth and death. The experience or viewpoint of an Enlightened being.

UPĀYA   The skilful methods compassionately employed by Buddhas and others to interest people in the Dharma and encourage them to follow the path to Enlightenment.

VAJRA   A ritual sceptre, which symbolically combines the qualities of both diamond and thunderbolt.

VAJRAYĀNA   The 'way of the diamond thunderbolt' – Buddhist Tantra (q.v.) of India and the Himalayan region.

VISUALIZATION   A common method of Buddhist meditation, involving the use of imagination to create vivid symbolic forms.

WHEEL OF LIFE   A graphic representation in one painting of the whole process through which craving, hatred, and ignorance cause living beings to circle in states of unsatisfactoriness. It includes depictions of the six realms of devas, asuras, humans, animals, hungry ghosts, and beings in hell (all q.v.), which together represent all the mental states unenlightened living beings can experience.

WISDOMS, FIVE   The Wisdoms of the five Jinas (q.v.): the Mirror-Like Wisdom, Wisdom of Equality, Discriminating Wisdom, All-Accomplishing Wisdom, and the Wisdom of the Dharmadhātu (sphere of reality).

YĀNA   A 'way' or 'vehicle' which can be used for attaining Buddhahood. One of the great streams of thought and teaching (embracing a number of schools) that have appeared in the development of Buddhism. (*See* Hīnayāna, Mahāyāna, Vajrayāna).

YIDAM (*Tibetan*) A Buddhist meditational deity embodying an aspect of Enlightenment. The term is sometimes reserved for meditational deities visualized in Highest Tantra (q.v.).

YOGA A Sanskrit word meaning union. In Buddhist Tantra it refers to a method of meditation or physical exercise designed to bring about spiritual development.

YOGĀCĀRA See Cittamātra.

YOGIN A male practitioner of yoga. The term is applied particularly to adepts of Buddhist Tantra.

YOGINĪ A female practitioner of yoga; a female Tantric adept.

ZEN (*Japanese*) A school of Mahāyāna Buddhism found mainly in Japan and Korea. 'Zen' is derived from the Sanskrit word *dhyāna* meaning meditation, and Zen places great emphasis on the practice of seated meditation. It aims not to rely on words and logical concepts for communicating the Dharma, often preferring to employ action or paradoxes.

Selected Reading

General

David L. Snellgrove, *Indo-Tibetan Buddhism*, Serindia, 1987.
Blanche Christine Olschak and Geshe Thupten Wangyal, *Mystic Art of Ancient Tibet*, Shambhala, 1987.
Marilyn M. Rhie and Robert A.E. Thurman, *The Sacred Art of Tibet*, Thames and Hudson, 1991.

Chapter One

H.W. Schumann, *The Historical Buddha*, Arkana, 1989.
Bhikkhu Ñāṇamoli, *The Life of the Buddha*, Buddhist Publication Society, 1978.
Voice of the Buddha, The Lalitavistara Sūtra (2 vols.), translated from the French by Gwendolyn Bays, Dharma Publishing, 1983.

Chapter Three

Kamalashila, *Meditation: The Buddhist Way of Tranquillity and Insight*, Windhorse Publications, 1996.
Kathleen McDonald, *How To Meditate*, Wisdom Publications, 1984.

Chapter Five

Giuseppe Tucci, *The Theory and Practice of the Mandala*, Rider, 1969.

Chapters Six to Ten

Lama Anagarika Govinda, *Foundations of Tibetan Mysticism*, Weiser Books, 1969.
Francesca Fremantle and Chögyam Trungpa, *The Tibetan Book of the Dead*, Shambhala, 1975.
Lati Rinbochay and Jeffrey Hopkins, *Death, Intermediate State and Rebirth*, Rider, 1979.
E.B. Cowell and others (eds.), *Buddhist Mahāyāna Texts*, Dover Publications, 1969.

Index

Windhorse Publications is a Buddhist publishing house, staffed by practising Buddhists. We place great emphasis on producing books of high quality, accessible and relevant to those interested in Buddhism at whatever level. Drawing on the whole range of the Buddhist tradition, our books include translations of traditional texts, commentaries, books that make links with Western culture and ways of life, biographies of Buddhists, and works on meditation.

As a charitable institution we welcome donations to help us continue our work. We also welcome manuscripts on aspects of Buddhism or meditation. To join our email list, leave your address on our website. For orders and catalogues log on to www.windhorsepublications.com or contact:

Windhorse Publications	Perseus Distribution	Windhorse Books
11 Park Road	1094 Flex Drive	P O Box 574
Birmingham	Jackson TN 38301	Newtown NSW 2042
B13 8AB	USA	Australia
UK		

Windhorse Publications is an arm of the Friends of the Western Buddhist Order, which has more than sixty centres on four continents. Through these centres, members of the Western Buddhist Order offer regular programmes of events for the general public and for more experienced students. These include meditation classes, public talks, study on Buddhist themes and texts, and bodywork classes such as t'ai chi, yoga, and massage. The FWBO also runs several retreat centres and the Karuna Trust, a fundraising charity that supports social welfare projects in the slums and villages of southern Asia.

Many FWBO centres have residential spiritual communities and ethical businesses associated with them. Arts activities are encouraged too, as is the development of strong bonds of friendship between people who share the same ideals. In this way the FWBO is developing a unique approach to Buddhism, not simply as a set of techniques, but as a creatively directed way of life for people living in the modern world.

If you would like more information about the FWBO please visit the website at www.fwbo.org or write to

London Buddhist Centre	Aryaloka	Sydney Buddhist Centre
51 Roman Road	14 Heartwood Circle	24 Enmore Road
London	Newmarket NH 03857	Sydney NSW 2042
E2 0HU	USA	Australia
UK		

ALSO FROM WINDHORSE PUBLICATIONS

The Breath
by Vessantara

The breath: always with us, necessary to our very existence, but often unnoticed. Yet giving it attention can transform our lives.

This is a very useful combination of practical instruction on the mindfulness of breathing with much broader lessons on where the breath can lead us. Vessantara, a meditator of many years experience, offers us:

- ⋆ Clear instruction on how to meditate on the breath
- ⋆ Practical ways to integrate meditation into our lives
- ⋆ Suggestions for deepening calm and concentration
- ⋆ Advice on how to let go and dive into experience
- ⋆ Insights into the lessons of the breath

The Breath returns us again and again to the fundamental and precious experience of being alive.

144 pages
ISBN 1 899579 69 9
£6.99/$10.95/€10.95

An interesting in depth investigation into the art of breathing.
Yoga magazine

The Heart
by Vessantara

The Heart offers ways to discover your emotional potential through an exploration of the practice of loving-kindness meditation.

Vessantara has practised this meditation for over thirty years. Here he shares his experience, gently encouraging us to unlock what is in our hearts and helping us to gain greater enjoyment from life. Among other benefits, using the exercises and meditations in this book you can:

- ⋆ Increase your emotional awareness
- ⋆ Feel more at ease with yourself
- ⋆ Become kinder and more open-hearted
- ⋆ Discover how to be more patient
- ⋆ Engage more spontaneously with life.

The Heart provides clear instruction and helpful suggestions for those new to meditation as well as more experienced practitioners.

176 pages
ISBN 9781 899579 71 6
£6.99/$10.95/€10.95

—the art of meditation series—

Buddhism: Tools for Living Your Life
by Vajragupta

This book is a guide for those seeking a meaningful spiritual path while living everyday lives full of families, work, and friends. Vajragupta provides clear explanations of Buddhist teachings and guidance applying these to enrich our busy and complex lives.

The personal stories, exercises, reflections, and questions in this book help transform Buddhist practice into more than a fine set of ideals. They make the path of ethics, meditation, and wisdom a tangible part of our lives.

In this book I have attempted to convey a feeling for what a 'Buddhist life' might be like – the underlying flavour, or ethos, of such a life. I hope I have made it clear that this way of life is possible for anyone – whatever their background and experience. My aim is to make the teachings as accessible and relevant as possible, and to give you some 'tools' with which to live a spiritual life.

"I'm very pleased that someone has finally written this book! At last, a real 'toolkit' for living a Buddhist life. His practical suggestions are hard to resist!"

Saddhanandi, Chair of Taraloka,
named Retreat Centre of the Year 2006 by *The Good Retreat Guide*

192 pages
ISBN 9781 899579 74 7
£10.99/$16.95/€16.95

Creative Symbols of Tantric Buddhism
by Sangharakshita

Tantric Buddhism is concerned with the direct experience of who we are and what we can become. For the Tantra this experience cannot be meditated by concepts, but it can be evoked with the help of symbols.

This is a thorough and informative introduction to:

* The symbolism of colour, mantras, and the mandala of the five Buddhas
* The Tibetan Wheel of Life – a map of our mind and emotions
* Figures of the Tantric tradition – Buddhas, Bodhisattvas, dakinis, and the archetypal guru
* The symbolism of ritual objects and offerings
* Confronting and transforming our fear of crisis situations and death

224 pages, with b&w illustrations
ISBN 1 899579 47 8
£10.99/$19.95/€19.95

FORTHCOMING BOOKS IN THIS SERIES

A Guide to the Bodhisattvas
by Vessantara

When we meet with one of the Bodhisattvas – whether in a painting or sculpture or visualized in meditation – we are brought face to face with a being that embodies Enlightenment. An encounter with such a figure is likely to move us far more deeply than a list of the qualities of someone who is enlightened. Bodhisattvas are dedicated to helping ordinary people on the path towards Enlightenment. This guide introduces a panoply of these figures from the vast array within the Buddhist tradition. In meeting Tārā, the rescuer, Mañjuśrī, the Bodhisattva of Wisdom, Avalokiteśvara, the Bodhisattva of Compassion, and many others, we become transformed by their qualities.

160 pages
11.99/$18.95/€18.95
ISBN 978 1 899579 84 6

A Guide to the Deities of the Tantra
by Vessantara

Tantric deities? Who are they and what do they do? This book provides a fascinating insight into a subject that has captivated the imagination of many but remains mysterious and exotic to all but a few. This volume focuses on the deities whose mantra recitation and colourful visualizations lie at the heart of the Tantra. We meet goddesses of wisdom, the prince of purity, the lotus-born guru Padmasambhava, and ḍākinīs – wild-haired women who dance in the flames of freedom. The peaceful and the wrathful urge the reader to break through to wisdom, pointing out the true nature of reality with uncompromising vigour.

172 pages
Price £11.99/$18.95/€18.95
ISBN 978 1 899579 85 3